FALL OF THE CRYPTO QUEEN

THE TRUE STORY OF HOW THE MISSING DR. RUJA IGNATOVA BUILT A CULT OF CRYPTO AND SCAMMED VICTIMS OUT OF BILLIONS

CHRIS KRAFFT

I DIGRESS

Copyright © 2023 by Chris Krafft. All rights reserved.

No portion of this book may be reproduced in any form without written permission from the publisher or author, except as permitted by copyright law.

FALL OF THE CRYPTO QUEEN

Prologue - The Queen and Her Con	1
Part 1 - One Coin, One Life: Listening for the Language of Fraud	7
1. "We Create the World"	9
2. The Cult and Its Queen	23
3. The Gospel of Gold	41
Part 2 - The Con and the Lie: Detecting the Machinery of Fraud	53
4. Weaponizing Hope	55
5. "There Is No Blockchain"	69
Part 3 - The Hunt for the Queen	87
6. Justice for Some	89
7. Most Wanted	97

Fall of the Crypto Queen

Prologue - The Queen and Her Con

ON THE NIGHT OF JUNE 11TH, 2016, THE WORLD was introduced to a queen.

She wasn't the queen of a nation, fan base, or beauty pageant. She was the queen of the new, wildly popular world of cryptocurrency. Instead of a crown, she wore gold and diamond earrings that glittered and sparkled about her. Instead of a robe, she donned a stunning red gown and striking crimson lipstick.

The queen marched onstage after a bloated introduction from her partner, bringing every occupant of London's Wembley Arena to their feet. Taking the microphone, she proceeded to teach the wonders of OneCoin, the world's first "mass market" cryptocurrency. While BitCoin was for the snooty elites of the technical world, OneCoin was accessible to anybody.

"In two years," she said, gazing boldly over the room, "no one will talk about BitCoin anymore." [1]

The crypto queen had spoken and the crowd responded with cheers and applause. What this woman said mattered. Her words seemed to be blessed with prophecy, and her followers were more devoted than ever.

Yet in less than two years, this infamous "queen" would be gone. Her name would no longer be spoken in reverence but derision. The billions she had persuaded people to invest in her cryptocurrency would be gone, too, vanished into dozens of accounts, properties, and yachts.

And everyone would still be talking about BitCoin.

Dr. Ruja Ignatova shocked the world with her new cryptocurrency in 2014, only to shock it once more by evanescing from public life like a ghost in October of 2017. In the intervening months and years, her circle of colleagues, advisors, and even family members have been arrested for a slough of international financial crimes. OneCoin has been outed for what it is and always was: A scam. Its offices have been raided and the business has been banned in practically every country in the world. [2] In a few short years Dr. Ruja, the queen of cryptocurrency, gathered an army of passionate followers, collected a fortune in swindled wealth, and disappeared with it.

When Dr. Ruja vanished and took her billions with her, she left thousands of destitute victims without any answers or recourse. It may be easy to dismiss these victims as Wall Street gamblers, suit-wearing hedge fund managers who had it coming. And while some of OneCoin's targets were among this elite class, the vast majority of victims were working class families. They were people who believed they were making a responsible decision with their hard-earned dollars, pounds, euros, yuan, and schillings.

Among its advocates, OneCoin wasn't just a cryptocurrency. It was a revolution that would "bank the unbanked." As Dr. Ruja often repeated, OneCoin was about bringing cryptocurrency to everyday workers and families who didn't have access to the high dollar trades on Wall Street.

Now that Ruja is gone and her currency revealed to be a sham, there has been little recourse for her victims. Criminal trials have indicted and even convicted some of its highest officers, but no lawsuits have yet yielded restitution. In other words, no one has been made whole. Families mortgaged houses, emptied savings accounts, and scraped together what little they had in exchange for what OneCoin was offering. It was nothing more than a massive con. All they can do now is try to find Dr. Ruja and bring her to justice.

While Ruja remains at large, there is some hope for her victims. In December 2022, partner and co-founder Karl Sebastian Greenwood pleaded guilty to wire fraud and money laundering. Her brother, Konstantin, has entered a similar plea and is currently cooperating with the United States government.[3]

An ominous detail lurks in the court filings. In exchange for cooperating with the FBI, Konstantin Ignatova will be placed in the Witness Protection Program. He claims he is concerned for the safety of himself, his family, and his closest friends. Furthermore, many former employees, promoters, and associates have refused to testify about OneCoin or will only do so under the condition of anonymity. Even though OneCoin's leadership is missing, dead, or behind bars, the real muscle behind it is not, causing people to legitimately fear for their lives. OneCoin wasn't just a smash and grab operation; it developed deep and intimate ties to organized crime and terrorism, and its leaders likely know too much for their own good. [4]

While Greenwood and Konstantin will receive protection for their compliance, Dr. Ruja has no such assurances. She could be practically anywhere—including in an unmarked grave.

Since Dr. Ruja's disappearance, authorities, journalists, podcasters, and millions of desperate victims have been trying to find her. Some, including those closest to her, believe Ruja has been dead for a long time. Others aren't so sure, having tracked her through numerous sightings, transactions, and rumors—breadcrumbs left by a shadow in hiding.

If she is among the living, there is little doubt it is by the grace and favor of some unsavory characters in the world of international business and organized crime. This is perhaps why, in June 2022, the FBI added Dr. Ruja to their "Most Wanted" list. She is only the eleventh woman to ever make the list, and this action only gins up more speculation that Dr. Ruja is alive *and* potentially within law enforcement's grasp. Details from the Bureau are few for obvious reasons, but the fact that Dr. Ruja is on the Top Ten list more than five years since her disappearance is a tantalizing prospect. [5]

Perhaps Dr. Ruja finally made enough mistakes to expose her secret life. If she were to be caught, her victims would finally have a chance to seek justice from the woman who sold them nothing but lies.

PROLOGUE - THE QUEEN AND HER CON

BEFORE HER EMPIRE WAS REVEALED TO BE A FRAUD, Dr. Ruja Ignatova seemed untouchable. She earned a doctorate in international law from the University of Constance and later worked for McKinsey and Company. Ignatova was rising to the top of an emerging market where finance and technology intersect, and in 2015 she graced the cover of Bulgaria's edition of *Forbes* and spoke at a forum for *The Economist*. Thousands of zealous followers hung on her every word, attended her events, and most importantly, bought into her new cryptocurrency.[6]

Yet the mass majority of OneCoin's "investors" knew little about how cryptocurrency works. Some knew nothing at all.

In spite of this, Ruja, Konstantin, and Sebastian Greenwood were able to convince people this didn't matter. OneCoin was the crypto for the masses. BitCoin had gone big time, and OneCoin was going to go even bigger.

The truth is that Ruja didn't need to explain cryptocurrency to make OneCoin what it was. She tapped into a more powerful force than even profit motive or greed. Instead, she found a way to build a new religion, and its adherents brought the same zeal as a member of any notorious cult. Across dozens of nations, Dr. Ruja shared her gospel of OneCoin and the OneLife network. Her message spread rapidly and fiercely, winning customers of all ethnicities and religions. From earthen huts of Uganda to cramped apartments of Beijing, OneCoin was everywhere. Its adherents were all in. They were proud to belong.

What Dr. Ruja and Greenwood perpetrated isn't new. This con has been repackaged and rebranded many times. In almost every way, it was Ponzi and Madoff with a fresh coat of digital paint.

How do scams like OneCoin end up so devilishly successful? How can average people protect themselves from schemes such as these?

This is not just the story of how Dr. Ruja Ignatova successfully swindled $4 billion and then evaporated like a ghost. It is the story of ordinary men and women like you and me.

Scams flood our communication channels everyday through our email accounts, phones, and social media profiles. Most of the time we can swipe and delete them with ease.

But what do we do when these false promises are on the lips of our closest loved ones? How can we defend ourselves? How can we discern the truth from the lies, especially when the topic is so new, cutting edge, and promising?

By examining OneCoin and its villainous founder, we can learn valuable lessons about modern frauds and how to avoid them. By hearing stories of victims who have been brave enough to share their experiences, we gain wisdom and strategies that protect us and our loved ones from would-be thieves. And by studying historical and psychological trends, we can spot patterns that almost always lead to fraud.

This is the story of Dr. Ruja Ignatova and OneCoin, one of the grandest scams in history, and how we can use its lessons to protect ourselves from whatever's coming next.

Part 1 - One Coin, One Life: Listening for the Language of Fraud

1

"WE CREATE THE WORLD"

MOST PEOPLE DON'T UNDERSTAND cryptocurrency. Frankly, most people don't need to understand it. At least not yet.

As of this writing, cryptocurrency is still on the fringe of the financial world. It is widely considered the riskiest of investment products given the fact that it is not regulated by any international governing body. It isn't tied to a particular nation or physical resource, like gold or precious gems. And for some, it's damned confusing.

For people who don't pay attention, crypto can seem like a subject largely reserved for single guys and businessmen who frequent high-end restaurants, sip craft beer or hard seltzer, and toss words around like "blockchain," "halving," and "NFTs." It's a fun curiosity, a human interest topic one can study like mountain climbers or ultra-marathon runners.

Yet for more and more investors, cryptocurrency is considered a legitimate investment to add to a portfolio, even if they don't really understand how it works. There have been several negative consequences of the mass-marketification of cryptocurrency, including fraud that targets people who don't understand how the digital sausage is getting made.

Many new crypto investors are primarily concerned with financial return, rather than sustainability and legitimacy. How those returns are generated may not be entirely clear, but when the possibility of immense returns is out there, some investors don't care about the pesky details and toss their money in anyway.

This phenomenon isn't exclusive to cryptocurrency. Many markets have risen from nowhere only to collapse a few short years later. The "Dot Com" bubble of the early 2000s is a prime example where investors overvalued short-term returns and undervalued long-term feasibility. This boom-and-bust cycle not only imperils naive investors; it invites the dishonest parties to join the game, take advantage of the frenzy, and make off with illegitimate gains.

This is exactly what OneCoin was able to do.

To fully understand what OneCoin did and appreciate the depth of its founders' depravity, we must first acquire a basic understanding of cryptocurrency and how it functions. Unless we dive into the details, we will never see the devil doing his dirty work in their midst.

What the Heck is Cryptocurrency?

If you've ever wondered what BitCoin is and why so many people are talking about it, you're not alone.

"WE CREATE THE WORLD" 11

Cryptocurrency is the new kid on the block, and those who know about it tend to be very excited. In the early 2010s, BitCoin burst onto the scene. Created a few years earlier by an online figure known as Satoshi Nakamoto in an online post titled "Bitcoin: A Peer to Peer Electronic Cash System," the first cryptocurrency was designed to redefine the fundamental notions of money.[1]

These first dialogues about digital cryptocurrency were relegated to the financial and technological niches of society. Yet within half a decade BitCoin exploded, and its earliest investors were handsomely rewarded for their good faith. Other cryptocurrencies like Etherium, Tether, and the meme-inspired DogeCoin have emerged as well. But the granddaddy of all digital currency remains BitCoin, and its name has achieved eponym status in the vein of Kleenex and Coke.

BitCoin has also gone bust several times over its history, thanks in part to a hefty number of scams and fraudulent companies. A recent example, the crypto exchange FTX, put a number of celebrities in hot water due to their endorsements of the brand. Like all assets, BitCoin rises and falls due to diverse market forces. And even though it is digital, BitCoin is limited in supply, just like cash, real estate, goods, services, and every other thing of tangible value. The process of "mining," or creating, new coins is also getting harder and more expensive.

Cryptocurrency upends much of what we traditionally think about currency: How its value is determined, who gets to make it, and how it is verified. To appreciate what Dr. Ruja Ignatova and her cohorts did, it's imperative to understand that real cryptocurrencies, like BitCoin, are limited in supply and cannot be "double spent," or used twice for the same transactions. It is different from "fiat" currency, or money minted by national treasuries, in that it isn't tied to a particular nation nor does it take physical form. In a sense it is like a debit card, which is connected to your bank's online network.

You can be forgiven for not knowing how all of this works. Unlike coins and cash, digital currency is particularly difficult to comprehend since there is no physical asset to picture in one's mind. The inner machinations of an entire decentralized network of computers working in cooperation don't lend themselves to the same visual renderings as a pile of coins or cash.

These innovations have had unintended negative side effects. Without government regulation and oversight, cryptocurrency moves around the globe anonymously. BitCoin and AltCoins (like Ethereum and the rest) are a gift to money launderers wishing to take real cash from illegal activities and transform it into something "clean." What's to stop drug cartels from depositing tens of millions of profits into a cryptocurrency and then withdrawing the funds in a fiat currency of choice? Since there is no governing body, no regulatory agency overseeing international digital transactions, there is essentially nothing standing in their way. [2]

While cryptocurrency is inherently borderless, it is not immune from the laws of nations where it is deposited or withdrawn. This is perhaps the only defense against illegal and immoral uses of digital currency, and it is an area where law enforcement must work hard to keep up with changing technology and methods.

There are several key differences that we will explore later, but for now this understanding will be sufficient to learn how Dr. Ruja began conning the world with her new cryptocurrency, OneCoin. The simplest explanation is that cryptocurrency is online money, and there are different kinds of it, just like the currencies of different nations. But instead of each currency being tied to its country, each is connected to a unique online record of every transaction that uses it. This record, as we'll soon learn, is called the Blockchain.

Riding a Wave of FOMO

When BitCoin blew up and poured Scrooge McDuck amounts of money on its earliest inventors, the financial world wanted in. Thus was born a new term: Crypto FOMO.

Fear of Missing Out, or FOMO, is a common psychological concept. Anytime someone makes a foolish or overly hasty decision because there is concern over missing out on an opportunity, they are acting out of FOMO.

Thanks to the speed with which BitCoin rose to prominence, it was an ideal candidate to create plenty of investment FOMO. People who missed the first wave understandably wished they'd had the foresight to see BitCoin as the next big thing. Without a doubt, many of these people still didn't understand what the heck crypto really *was*. That wasn't going to stop them from chasing a big payday.
[3]

Even for the uneducated, most investments make relative sense if explained well. Mortgage bonds are large portfolios of home loans. Commodities are raw materials that rarely differ regardless of who is growing or harvesting them. Company stocks are interwoven with the success or failure of that particular business. These investments don't cause a big fuss in the global economy, which is why they are so popular.

These investments are also somewhat boring and infrequently create a rush of FOMO in the general public. A company can come along and cause wild fluctuations from time to time, like Tesla or Apple or even Gamestop, but these are rare byproducts of human unpredictability. FOMO is reserved for the most complicated and risky investments.

Take the housing crash of 2008. While it was caused by mortgage bonds, the real culprits were illegal lending practices that preyed on the desperate or ignorant. Home buyers were tricked into signing loans with adjustable rate mortgages on properties they couldn't afford. Many were immigrants who spoke little to no English. Others were greedy speculators hoping to capitalize on the rapidly accelerating housing market. The housing FOMO was real.

When the adjustable rates kicked in, mortgage defaults went through the roof. Soon the bonds made up of these loans had no actual value. Billions in retirements and pensions vanished.

This wasn't all. Since home loans were considered such airtight investments, banks began selling speculative products based on the success of the bonds—synthetic CDOs, or collateralized debt obligations—meaning even more money would disappear if the bonds failed. When all was said and done, trillions of dollars that were riding on the housing market simply doing what it always seemed to do went up in smoke.

In spite of this, there were a few hedge funds that made out well: Firms that dared to bet that the housing market would fail. To do this, another type of investment was invented out of thin air, an investment that some might consider unethical or mildly dangerous. In a nutshell, these fearless investors "shorted" the mortgage bonds and ended up making hundreds of millions while the rest of society was on fire.

These smart and lucky few are the exception to the rule; yet those who are exceptional are immortalized in story and film. This is perhaps why FOMO can quickly go viral: It depends on the success of so few to spread to so many. [4]

The same can be said of BitCoin's sudden rise. For the few who were lucky enough to get in early, BitCoin yielded an incredible profit. This created a new kind of FOMO around cryptocurrency that was especially difficult for some to pass up. It was, and for some still is, new and thrilling.

But it is terribly risky, making it different from a new company or mortgage bond. Yes, risk is inherent in any investment, and there is simply no such thing as a "sure thing" when it comes to Wall Street. That doesn't stop people from looking for risk-free investments, or from claiming to sell them.

When Dr. Ruja swept onto the scene in 2014 and began hawking OneCoin as "the future of payments" and the world's first "mass market cryptocurrency," people paid attention. OneCoin events popped up across Great Britain, Bulgaria, and Germany, the founder appearing bedecked in stunning ball gowns and shimmering jewelry. She arrived on time and fully prepared for her presentations. Her full lips glowed ruby red and her diamond earrings twinkled under the stage lights as she explained how OneCoin was going to change the world.

Some will say that it was obvious from the start that OneCoin was a scam, but these people are either intricately knowledgeable about cryptocurrency or just enjoying the buoyancy of hindsight.

A blatant scam or not, OneCoin looked like something that had to be talked about. Its queen was brilliant and beautiful. She was a doctor who had worked for McKinsey and Co. OneCoin allegedly had all the same elements as its main competitor—online payments, blockchain, rapid growth—but it was for regular people, not just the wealthy and elite. Its branding was sleek, its events spectacular. OneCoin wasn't just a new cryptocurrency. It was going to be a new way of life. [5]

As a tidal wave of crypto FOMO was sweeping across the globe in 2014, Dr. Ruja Ignatova and her partner, Karl Sebastian Greenwood, plotted exactly how to leverage it to reap a harvest of unthinkable wealth. To make her new cryptocurrency practically a household name, Dr. Ruja adopted a clever—and nefarious—angle. She made her cryptocurrency a movement.

OneCoin's marketing didn't discuss the matters of mining, encrypting, and decentralizing; it didn't need to. Its YouTube channel (which is still published) features video clips of its events, and you won't see people on computers tinkering with the machinery of actual cryptocurrency.

Instead, you'll see something akin to a religious event or a rock concert. Emcees fire up crowds. Lights flash, pop songs blare, and fireworks burst into the air like gold confetti. When the camera pans through the crowd, one might see people holding up a hand to make an "O" with their thumb and forefinger. This was the OneCoin sign, and it meant you were part of a special community, known lovingly as the OneLife *family*. [6]

OneCoin wasn't successful because it was about cryptocurrency. Instead, it made itself into a place to Believe and to Belong. By weaponizing these two fundamental human motivations, Dr. Ruja was able to steal over $4 billion from people who had the utmost faith in her.

Sure, they didn't know much about cryptocurrency.

But from their point of view, they didn't need to. They had Dr. Ruja, and that was all that mattered.

"Some of You Have Children"

During the 2016 event at Wembley Arena, Dr. Ruja held the crowd of 90,000 in the palm of her hand as she extolled the virtues of an exclusive community called the OneLife Network. One of the perks of this community, of course, was that everyone who joined was going to be exceedingly rich.

Exactly *how* this was going to happen, however, was never explained. It didn't need to be. Everything looked so beautiful, so convincing, so *successful*, there didn't seem to be much reason to question.

"She looked like a queen," recalled Igor Alberts. One of OneCoin's most successful promoters, Alberts met Ruja Iganatova in 2015 and was immediately impressed with her.

He brought his entire sales network to the company and soon began making piles of money in the name of OneCoin.

Speaking to journalist and host Jamie Bartlett on his groundbreaking BBC podcast *The Missing CryptoQueen*, Alberts explained why he was so eager to be a part of Ignatova's new cryptocurrency. It was all about "the big change" and creating a "second bank tier" for those without access to banking and investments to get access to larger sources of wealth.[7]

At Wembley, Ruja thrilled her audience with bold promises about future success, referring to a simple but persuasive slideshow on the massive screen behind her. The talk used the perfect blend of crypto buzzwords and jargon to keep OneCoin's investors convinced of its legitimacy. She told an immensely satisfying story, and millions of people literally bought it.

"We are more than just OneCoin," she said, her scarlet dress trailing behind her. "We create the world around this coin. And this is what our network does. Not only mining the coin, but creating a whole ecosystem."

That ecosystem was the OneLife Network. On the screen behind Ruja, a circular graphic appeared with the word "OneCoin" in the middle. Sprouting out from this were slices of the pie, each with its own word describing part of the network: "Charity," "Partnerships," and "Payments" to name a few.

And at the top, right where 1:00 might be on a clock, the graph read, "Education."

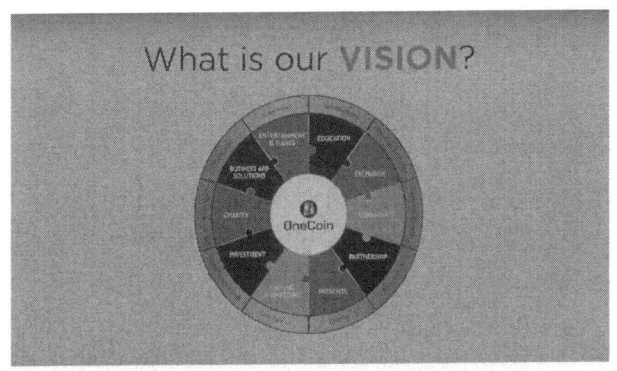

Ignatova, Dr. Ruja and One Coin.
"The Blockchain," YouTube, 11 July
2016. https://www.youtube.com/watch?v=638
_Jpp2Rq8&t=1980s&ab_channel=OneCoin

For anyone in attendance looking for signs of a scam, this should have been the first red flag. While "Education" may seem an innocent term, it is often code for propaganda. It is also a way to dodge skepticism and claims of fraud.

"OneCoin for me always starts with education," Dr. Ruja continued. "Some of you have children. So at one point these children want to drive a car. Would you let your child drive a car without a driver's license, without knowing the rules, without knowing what a car is? I would not."

For any scammer, a key challenge is to overcome the prospect's doubts. The highly technical details of cryptocurrency were certainly a potential barrier for prospective OneCoin investors. But for Dr. Ruja, this problem actually provided a chance to assuage any concerns or questions about the legitimacy of her product. The disadvantages of cryptocurrency quickly became a malevolent advantage. That's why OneCoin technically sold education, not coins.

It wasn't possible to buy OneCoins directly. Instead, investors purchased educational packages that purportedly taught everything there was to know about cryptocurrency. These materials were sold in various sizes, some in the mere hundreds of dollars or euros, others, like the "Tycoon" package, in the thousands. Only when a buyer was grafted into this education system, dubbed the OneAcademy, did they receive "tokens" to mine coins. This mining happened behind the scenes, and while members of the OneLife community didn't know what, if anything, was going on in that "mining," they had little reason to worry. All they had to do was log onto a website and watch the value of these "coins" constantly go up in price day after day.

Yet there was every reason to worry because this value was completely made up. There were no actual coins that could be bought, sold, or traded. What investors saw on their screens was the product of a computer program mimicking the behavior of a real cryptocurrency's value in the real global marketplace. [8]

"I see the OneAcademy as a kind of driver's license for cryptocurrency," Dr. Ruja explained, further disarming skeptics in the audience. "Do not mine cryptocurrency [and] do not trade cryptocurrency without education, because it is one of the riskiest investment classes out there and you have to know what to do."

This line is painfully ironic. It worked perfectly to support the con by claiming to protect its victims from other scams, a classic move by any experienced abuser. In a world with so many wolves, Dr. Ruja was able to convince everyone that she was the shepherd guarding the sheep. OneCoin wasn't just digital currency; it was a safe haven, and it cared about you and your children.

It comes as no surprise that OneCoin's educational materials were found to be plagiarized. The information in these materials was also not helpful enough to teach investors that their cryptocurrency investment was all a sham. Despite the lies, the copyright infringement, and the fraud, Dr. Ruja put the elements in place to execute a massive con and get away with it, at least for a few years. [9]

The harvest was ripe for reaping, as crypto FOMO crippled the judgment and emotional temperament of many investors. Questions and concerns about new cryptocurrencies certainly abounded, but Ruja seemed to have all the answers.

Not sure how cryptocurrency works?

We'll teach you.

Worried about losing your investment?

Just look at how well BitCoin is doing—and we're doing it better.

I'm still not sure about joining some crypto group.

OneLife isn't about cryptocurrency or technology at all. It's about being one family and one community, and how everyone can have a better life by going cashless with OneCoin.

Dr. Ruja Ignatova's scam was successful because it sold more than an online product. It delivered solutions to fundamental human emotions. OneLife wasn't a business; it was a family. OneCoin wasn't money; it was saving the world from corruption and greed.

To pull this off, the perpetrators had to sacrifice much of their own humanity. Dr. Ruja gladly acknowledged that her victims had children of their own by tapping into parental empathy, only to use it to con bread-winners out of the resources they needed to support those very children. The ruse was equal parts despicable and effective, primarily because it wasn't about cryptocurrency, but trust.

That's why it worked so brilliantly.

In spite of so much success, OneCoin wasn't without its early detractors. Even in 2014, financial watch dogs, journalists, and crypto bloggers were suggesting that something wasn't right. It wasn't behaving like a cryptocurrency, but a pyramid scheme. Some even dared to suggest it might be a fraud.

Once again, Dr. Ruja had an answer.

That answer doomed her followers into abandoning all logic. All that mattered was their new OneLife family. Outsiders were shunned and silenced. Critics were treated as mortal enemies.

And many victims, outraged at the way the world was persecuting them and their crypto queen, would respond by buying even more packages, showing their absolute faith in times of trouble.

Dr. Ruja Ignatova created a world for herself. In this world, she was the matriarch, the queen, and the deliverer, and her followers were ready to die for her.

OneCoin had become a religion, and she was its messiah.

2

THE CULT AND ITS QUEEN

WHEN CAROLINE BROWN DECIDED TO LEAVE HER church, she knew there would be consequences. People would cut her off. Some might even spread lies about her.

But she didn't expect her daughter to never speak to her again.

Divorced and living a thousand miles from her children, Brown decided to depart the Church of Scientology in order to move home and be closer to her family. When she did so, her children immediately sent letters giving her the worst possible news: She was now a Suppressed Person.

A religion obsessed with shutting out negative worldly influences, Scientology requires its adherents to associate only with those who are deemed friendly to the cause. When loved ones and friends decide to leave the church, they are shunned and marked with an unforgivable brand. Only by returning to Scientology and undergoing hours and hours of expensive "clearing" can they be redeemed.

As reported by the Orlando Sentinel, Brown feared that she'd lost both her children forever. By a miracle, she re-established contact with her son, and now has a healthy relationship with him despite separating from her old faith. Her daughter, however, remains steadfast in her beliefs and refuses to associate with her mother, now a loathed SP in the eyes of the Church. [1]

Caroline's pain is unspeakable, but it isn't rare. For hundreds of ex-Scientologists, this is the new normal, and there are dozens of broken marriages, families, and communities as a result. Cults like the Church of Scientology live and die by the devotion of their followers. Gray areas are not allowed and nuance has little place in such an association.

For investors in OneCoin, a similar cult-like atmosphere pervaded every element of the experience. Buying into OneCoin wasn't just a financial decision, it was a lifestyle that guaranteed it would usher its people into a promised land of comfort, success, and generational wealth.

Like so many others, this cult had a charismatic and powerful leader: Dr. Ruja. When she spoke, it was as if God was making his will known on Earth.

And anyone who doubted her had to be suppressed and silenced, just like Caroline Brown.

Haters

The call came from an American number that Jen McAdam had never heard of before. The conversation didn't go well. Within minutes, McAdam was in tears while her caller was urging her to believe him when he said that OneCoin was a scam.

A Glasgow mother seeking to lift her family into a new era of financial prosperity, McAdam had invested tens of thousands of her own English pounds into OneCoin after participating in a webinar about the new cryptocurrency.

"The people were uptempo, full of passion, very, very passionate, [and said] how their lives have changed," McAdam told The Missing CryptoQueen podcast. "OneCoin... it's a family — [they used] very family-oriented words." [2]

Impressed by the presentation and Dr. Ruja's credentials, McAdam decided to buy her first package. A week later, she bought more. Within weeks, the delighted and hopeful woman had persuaded family and friends to deposit a whopping quarter-of-a-million British pounds into the cryptocurrency. They all believed they had just transformed their loved ones' lives forever.

Then Timothy Curry called.

A noted cryptocurrency enthusiast, Timothy Curry is an advocate for online currency and its potential to make the world a better place. But unlike the vast majority of OneCoin's investors, Curry understands how cryptocurrency is supposed to work, and spends much of his free time fighting the lies of criminals like Dr. Ruja.

"OneCoin is a scam," Curry declared over McAdam's despondent sobs, "and I can prove it."

Still, McAdam refused to shift her beliefs. How could she? Her family's well being depended on OneCoin and its promised salvation. [3]

To McAdam, Curry was just a Hater. Anyone who had criticism for OneCoin, the OneLife Network, or Dr. Ruja

Ignatova was just that: A Hater, a toxic-minded simpleton who refused to see the grandeur of what was happening in the world of digital finance. Even Jamie Barlett and the BBC have been recipients of this insular jargon, as in 2019 OneCoin attempted to counter the podcast's claims by saying, "It is OneCoin's aim to expand the markets and the possibilities of Onecoin's fungibility.... Trading is slowed down by authorities, regulators, and haters." [4]

Just like Scientology with its practice of hurling Suppressed Persons from its community, OneCoin's leadership sternly refused to tolerate any dissent whatsoever. Journalists who questioned OneCoin's legitimacy were branded as hucksters and frauds publishing unsubstantiated lies. Proponents of rival cryptocurrencies, OneCoin jeered, were just jealous of OneCoin's rapid success. They worked for the Big Banks and were terrified of the coming crypto revolution.

For millions of OneCoin investors like Jen McAdam, this circle-the-wagons attitude encouraged her to remain loyal and trust that her faith would soon be rewarded. But as the months and years carried on, and the thousands of euros McAdam and her loved ones invested remained out of hand, she began to grow restless. With restlessness came the willingness to defy her fellow crypto cultists, and before long she was the recipient of foul and heinous threats that won't be reprinted here.

In a way, it's understandable that people fiercely defend their tribes when threatened. Human alliances are inherently built on an "us vs. them" mentality. It fuels sports fandoms, politics, and patriotism. In many ways it is the bedrock of familial love.

Yet when "we" are commanded to deny the validity, humanity, and dignity of "them," red flags should begin to wave. Cults constantly feel the need to reinforce their front lines and convince their adherents that the lives of others aren't just "different," but heinous, sinful, and even Satanic. A loved one can become a devil with shocking rapidity.

The Cult of Crypto

Dr. Janja Lalich has dedicated herself to the mission of educating and liberating others. A survivor of a cult herself, Lalich's organization was a politically extremist one, the Democratic Workers Party. It took a decade for her to realize that everything she was being taught and pressured to do was an elaborate lie before she drummed up the courage to leave. [5]

"Concerted efforts at influence and control lie at the core of cultic groups, programs, and relationships," Lalich writes in her book *Take Back Your Life: Recovering from Cults and Abusive Relationships*. "Many members, former members, and supporters of cults are not fully aware of the extent to which members may be manipulated, exploited, or even abused."

Not all cults are identical, and some focus more intently on certain elements. However, Dr. Lalich's research can lead one to make a bold case that OneCoin and the OneLife Network fit the description of a modern cult. Among other descriptors, Lalich lists the following traits as indicative of cult-like control:

"The group displays an excessively zealous and unquestioning commitment to its leader.... Questioning, doubt, and dissent are discouraged or even punished.... The group is elitist, claiming a special, exalted status for itself, its leader(s), and its members.... The group has a polarized, us-versus-them mentality, which may cause conflict with the wider society.... The group is preoccupied with bringing in new members... [and] with making money. The most loyal members...often fear reprisals to themselves or others if they leave—or even consider leaving—the group." [6]

When Jen McAdam and other investors began to share their concerns about OneCoin, the ostracization quickly began.

"As soon as you buy your first package, you're entered into a OneCoin WhatsApp group," McAdam described. "If you've any negativity, you should not be in this group. You're told not to believe anything from the outside world... [or] haters. BitCoin. Even Google. Don't listen to Google. [Outsiders] are evil, they're bad. You're brainwashed. It's so cult-like." [7]

The moment McAdam began doubting, she committed the great sin of OneCoin. She became a Hater and deserved to be punished.

A cult's entire existence is predicated on eliminating all criticism. It must do so because the its founding principles and doctrines cannot hold up to sustained scrutiny. After too many questions and observations, the cult's doctrines and ideology almost certainly fall apart, as they are usually underpinned by unsubstantiated myths, claims, or cultural norms. This is likely because the cult is often one and the same with its founder.

Timothy Curry, the crypto advocate who pursued McAdam with the truth, explained his take on the cult-like structure of OneCoin: "Ruja is a doctor, double PhD. If you look at the top leaders, the way they dressed, the way they showed things off… they really did create a worship behind her. People would be like 'Bless you Ruja, God bless you.' It became worship." [8]

For early Scientologists, challenges to its belief system were a direct repudiation of L. Ron Hubbard and everything Hubbard claimed about the nature of life, death, and human suffering. For Dr. Lalich's Democratic Workers Party, everything flowed from the persona of its leader, Marlene Dixon, who allegedly ruled her political body like a demagogue and heaped abuse and insults on anyone who didn't obey her. It is ironic that like Ruja Ignatova, Dixon earned a PhD prior to building her cult, and these credentials no doubt added to her status as an individual above questioning. [9]

There are simply too many cult leaders to study in this discussion, yet they all share numerous traits, including a shocking lack of human empathy.

Stalin, Mao, Amin, Hubbard, Jones, or Ignatova: Each and every one lacked a compassionate sense of how their actions affected others. Dictators and cult leaders tend to see their members as little more than capital in an elaborate enterprise. Members are dollars to be collected and spent as needed.

Yet their language is rife with the rhetoric of love.

"OneCoin is for everyone. This is who we are: Global citizens of a small world, wanting to make a change," Ruja declared to her adoring followers at Wembley. She was considered the matriarch of OneCoin, yet giving birth to the company failed to endow her with actual motherly compassion.[10]

Like so many other cult leaders, Dr. Ruja was solely fixated on accumulating money. These figureheads find ways to blend faith and finance, transforming the beliefs of their marks into revenue streams. To question this becomes heresy, and such heresies threaten the standing of the cult leader. It's no wonder that doubters are excommunicated with great force and speed.

A former OneCoin employee spoke to *The Missing CryptoQueen* about OneCoin's central offices in Sofia, Bulgaria: "It's set up almost like a cathedral," the person said, sharing anonymously through a voice actor. "You don't speak out loud, you whisper to each other. Everything is gilded."[11]

It's no wonder OneCoin's most passionate devotees refused to listen to the critics. They weren't just members of a gym or contributors to an exciting crowd-sourced product. They were changing the world. They were a part of something important, something that would reward their faith and devotion by making them wildly rich.

And their savior, Dr. Ruja Ignatova, was leading the way, weathering an onslaught of international skepticism and accusations. How could she *not* be likened to a coming messiah, the misunderstood preacher, teacher, and sacrificial lamb who was ushering in a new kingdom? To an outsider, Dr. Ruja's outsider status, the golden offices in Sofia, the hand gestures, and the fierce insularity incite skepticism. But to the insider, one who has been "saved" by OneCoin, they are a sign of deliverance and no one is going to tell them otherwise.

The Bitch of Wall Street Meets MLM

OneCoin would never have become a money-making juggernaut without a king to accompany the crypto queen. That someone was Karl Sebastian Greenwood.

Ignatova and Greenwood met several years before the launch of OneCoin when they worked for a now-defunct cryptocurrency known as BigCoin. While Ignatova possessed the business and financial chops to run her own company, Greenwood had an idea that would set OneCoin apart: Multi-level marketing.

You've most likely heard of multi-level marketing, or MLM. You've possibly been invited to a pitch. The event begins like a casual night of fun with friends before it suddenly transforms into a sales talk for some miracle product, like dietary supplements, oxygenizing wine, or even medicinal marijuana. There is never a shortage of new, seemingly impressive products to sell in your living room to a circle of loved ones who you then invite to join their local business empire.

And that's the catch: No one in MLM *just* sells these things. Instead, the ultimate goal is to recruit a few friends or family members to join the company and start selling too. Once their loved ones start making sales, the recruiter gets a portion of the profits. This is called "downline" commissions.

The problem, as millions of would-be millionaires have discovered, is that after several generations of recruitment the MLM scheme becomes unsustainable. Prospects dry up, especially when the sponsoring company isn't developing new products to generate repeat sales. This is why so few companies are able to implement this strategy in a legitimate manner. Doing so requires restrained, prudent design that accommodates the system's inherent flaws.

MLM has earned a bad rap and has acquired a nickname that comes from the triangle-shaped plot of downline recruitment: "Pyramid scheme." All pyramid schemes aren't automatically frauds, and there are a few companies that execute the sales strategy with success like Mary Kay, Avon, and Amway.

But most do not, making pyramid schemes a generally unwise use of time and money for people looking for a leg up. The reason is simple: Economics.

The farther down the pyramid one is—in other words, if you join the network much later than everyone else—the more difficult it will be to sell. This yields few, if any, profits. It's no surprise then that most MLM companies are considered scams, even if they don't fit the technical definition of a fraudulent enterprise. Very few people in the company actually make any money, and those that do are concentrated at the top of the pyramid.

Greenwood saw the potential of MLM to make Ignatova's cryptocurrency business wildly successful. While MLM can generate a lot of skepticism, at least in well-developed countries with widespread access to the internet, many communities are insulated and cut off from the ability to research. Immigrants, as well as ethnic and religious minorities, often depend on one another for advice rather than the internet. To the average person, a multi-level marketing scheme may seem like a ridiculous investment.

But for millions of OneCoin victims, it was presented as an amazing opportunity to provide for themselves, their families, and their marginalized neighbors.

Greenwood's real stroke of genius wasn't just to build the business on MLM, but to hitch it to the worldwide flood of crypto FOMO. Hard-working families had a chance to be just like the Wall Street hotshots who got wind of the best deals before everyone else. It was their turn to strike gold. They may have missed the BitCoin rush, but they were just in time for something better. [12]

OneCoin promoters traveled to every corner of the Earth to spread the good financial news. After convincing prospects to buy education packages, they then encouraged these new investors to become promoters themselves. Their targets were some of the poorest people on the planet living in countries that lack financial oversight, insurance, and protections that many Americans and Europeans enjoy. Other victims lived on the fringes of developed countries, trying to balance old traditions with new culture and fast-paced technology.

When Greenwood suggested the scheme to Ignatova, she loved the idea and emailed him back: "The bitch of Wall Street meets MLM," a reference to the infamous "Wolf of Wall Street," Jordan Belfort. This message is one of many smoking guns exposing OneCoin as a blatant scam from the beginning. It was never an honest attempt to create a new cryptocurrency that somehow went sideways and devolved into something else. Indeed, recent court documents make it abundantly clear how Ignatova and Greenwood felt about their investors, as Ruja called their faux currency "trashy coin," while Greenwood referred to buyers as "idiots" in several emails. [13]

From day one, OneCoin was an elaborate deception aimed at stealing every penny it could find.

With their idea formed, Ignatova and Greenwood launched OneCoin in 2015 and began selling their education packages, complete with tokens to supposedly mine the new currency. The earliest adopters took possession of the top slots on the OneCoin pyramid, and from that point forward the race was on. With promises of gold raining down, new prospects were told that coins were selling fast and the price would only go up. Prospects *had* to buy now or risk missing out on a special, "risk-free" opportunity.

And if they felt any doubt or entertained a trickle of skepticism, there was the beautiful, picture-perfect founder: *Doctor* Ruja Ignatova, the prophetess of OneCoin, to reassure them.

A False Prophetess

Dr. Ruja Ignatova was born in Sofia, Bulgaria, in 1980. At an early age she wowed her teachers with her ambition and staggering intelligence. Her family relocated to Germany in the early 1990s where she grew into a young woman who enjoyed fashion and luxurious living. She studied at a variety of universities before earning a doctorate from Oxford, a detail that has shocked many of her doubters. Despite rumors to the contrary, Dr. Ruja *did* in fact earn a doctorate in business.

Her work in legitimate business was short and unexceptional. After serving with McKinsey for a brief period, she and her father decided to buy a German factory, the Waltenhofen Steelworks, which was on the brink of bankruptcy. At first, the arrangement seemed like a dream for hundreds of blue collar workers in the village of Allgäu. These men and women depended on the steel factory as it formed the lifeblood of the community's economy. When the Ignatovas took over, the townspeople were confident that a new era of prosperity had dawned on their little province.

But the new management began to make strange decisions that confused and frustrated the workers. Ruja and her father were rarely seen on the property, despite being familiar and friendly faces during the first years of ownership. Accounting books would vanish for days at a time and then reappear, their numbers heavily doctored. Workers arrived to find entire production lines shut down and inoperative; apparently large pieces of equipment had been sold in the night, rendering the factory practically useless.

In 2012, the Ignatovas sold the company without any warning. Employees were not informed of the sale and the new owners immediately filed for bankruptcy. The factory closed and the entire staff was laid off. While workers were livid, they were mostly heartbroken.

In hindsight, regulators and critics have come to believe that the Ignatovas purchased the company purely to embezzle its cash flow while selling it off bit by bit, juicing every available resource before tossing the rind to the side of the road.

The affair wasn't without consequences. In 2016, both Ruja and her father were summoned to a German courtroom to account for their misdeeds. Both pleaded guilty to embezzlement, bank fraud, and fraudulent accounting practices. Ruja's 14-month prison sentence was suspended for reasons unknown, and the crypto queen swiftly departed the country. [14]

For those keeping track, this conviction occurred in the midst of OneCoin's stellar run, the same year as Ruja's dramatic speech to thousands in Wembley Arena. At the same time the founder of a new cryptocurrency was pleading guilty to fraud-related crimes, swarms of global citizens were pouring billions into the OneCoin scheme due to their belief in that founder's genius.

Why wasn't this legal decision more widely reported? Why weren't investors warned that their cultish messiah had just been convicted of numerous frauds?

This lack of reporting and accountability is a direct byproduct of dealing in the widely unregulated space of international digital currency. There are few watch dogs, meaning the wolves can feast at will. Much can be said about the ineptitudes and evils of government, depending on one's preference of political system, but as OneCoin and other scams have shown, a broken system offers more protection than no system at all.

However, the blame cannot be entirely laid on the lack of regulation. Dr. Ruja's conviction was an unlikely candidate for press attention, as it lacked the appeal of a juicy crime or sensational victim. Whatever reports did emerge were likely drowned by the flash and bombast of the OneCoin media machine.

This, too, is a tactic of many cults: Flood the airwaves with positive coverage to drown any criticism. Dr. Ruja skillfully raised an army of dedicated zealots, all of whom trusted that she was about to deliver them to a land of financial milk and honey. Followers worshiped her and critics failed to pierce her bubble of influence. When opposing voices tried to convince devotees to abandon the cause, they refused to hear it. They suppressed dissent and shouted down the haters.

Rise of a Queen

Branding is everything.

One cannot know if Ruja Ignatova always intended to run scams on an unsuspecting world. One can, however, appreciate the accouterments of success with which Ignatova adorned herself, paving a gilded path toward glory and success.

The importance of her title, *Doctor*, cannot be understated. These honorifics are difficult to earn and worthy of respect. The term evokes considerable *ethos* and does a great deal to ward off suspicion or skepticism. Whether or not she earned her doctorate for the express purpose of leveraging it as a tool of deception is unknown; however, it did the job admirably, especially with investors who did their due diligence like Jen McAdam.

If the appellation of *Doctor* made her trustworthy, the title of *Queen* made her messianic.

It wasn't an epithet she came by on her own. In the late 2000s, Ruja befriended an Icelandic businesswoman and mainstay of the modeling world, Ásdís Rán. They went into business together as co-owners of a fashion boutique, The Ice Cave, located in Sofia. Due to Rán's incredible success on the runway, she had earned the nickname The Ice Queen. The two entrepreneurs worked together for several years until the store closed in 2011 and Rán returned to Iceland. Even with her friend departing, the term stuck in Ruja's mind.

When Ignatova founded OneCoin with Greenwood, the inspiration became reality. Ignatova knew exactly how to position herself in the crypto world, and did so quite easily. She wasn't just *Dr.* Ruja.

She was the Crypto*Queen.*

Throughout OneCoin's run, Ásdís Rán continued to stick close to her BFF. According to Icelandic journalist Auðr Ösp, "When Ruja established OneCoin in her home country, she contacted Ásdísi Rán and got her to work for the company. Among other things, Ásdís Rán was made the face of the electronic coin and was given the task of organizing luxury parties where the activities and the possibilities for investors to make huge sums of money were presented."

Since Ignatova's disappearance in 2017, Rán has been quick to articulate that she was never involved in the illegal aspects of OneCoin. She doesn't even seem to have been aware of the cryptocurrency's inherent fraudulence, stating in November of 2019: "[Ruja and Konstantin] are not criminals. Now I am in this family with her, her brother and everyone. They're just normal people who had a crazy good idea that did so incredibly well and went worldwide in one, two years." [15]

Ásdís Rán has returned to her own affairs, largely forgotten by the world of cryptocurrency and OneCoin investors. But her friendship with Ruja, and her royal title, inspired the leader of OneCoin to assume an almighty place in the public eye. To execute her scam—to truly pull off one of the greatest heists in global history—Ruja Ignatova needed to become more than just a savvy businesswoman.

She had to become regal, a leader by divine appointment.

With her elevated status secured, Ruja sat by her partner, Greenwood, and watched the money roll in. While she was married to a German lawyer, she began an affair with Greenwood, one of several that would play a significant role in her eventual downfall and disappearance. [16]

Meanwhile OneCoin promoters began spreading the "good news" to every corner of the Earth. Their message found listeners who had never heard of cryptocurrency and had practically no means to defend themselves against the con.

With vulnerable targets waiting, the OneCoin wolves set out for the hunt, eager to devour more victims and ingest them into their dear leader's cult of crypto.

3

THE GOSPEL OF GOLD

EVERY SUNDAY MORNING IN THE UGANDAN capital of Kampala, "Bishop" Fred Ntabazi opened the doors of his church on the fifth floor of the Padre Pio Building, eager to preach the gospel.

As the lead pastor of One Light International Ministries, Ntabazi stood before his faithful congregants and led hours of praise songs and worship. He preached about the goodness of God and prayed for the unity of all Ugandans. His followers spoke in exuberant tongues while Ntabazi stood by and lifted his hands in adulation.

If there was a place to hear the good news, this was clearly it.

For many attendees, the lesson had a uniquely monetary call to action. Instead of "passing of the plate," Bishop Ntabazi enjoined his worshipers to invest in a very specific company: OneCoin.

"OneCoin!" Pastor Fred would cry into his microphone.

"OneLife!" replied the invigorated congregation.

"*OneCoin!*" he repeated.

"*OneLife!*"

In late 2020, Bishop Fred Ntabazi delivered his last sermon. After running numerous Ponzi schemes on his congregants, Ntabazi's luck began to run out and he vanished. Local reporters speculate he is being protected by high-ranking officials in Ugandan law enforcement, given how quickly and efficiently Ntabazi was able to evade capture.

Regardless of where he is, or whether or not he is still alive, billions of Ugandan shillings are missing and likely to never be recovered.[1]

It comes as no surprise that Ntabazi was one of Uganda's most influential and financially successful OneCoin promoters. Until the government got wise to OneCoin's fraudulent nature, Ntabazi pushed the gospel of gold on his congregants and pressured them to buy for the sake of their salvation. According to numerous reports, some of his followers sold their houses to finance their OneCoin investments.

Ntabazi, meanwhile, was swift to enjoy the fruits of his labor and lived quite the lavish existence thanks to his elevated status on the OneCoin pyramid. Prior to his disappearance, Ntabazi drove a Land Rover in a country where the average annual household income is approximately $1,340.[2]

But now he is gone, vanished into the same air as Dr. Ruja Ignatova, and he left very few leads to help investigators track him down.

A Father's Trust

We've already explored the nature of cults and how they tend to extort their followers. Bishop Ntabazi is perhaps the purest embodiment of the OneCoin cult of wealth. It's possible he believed, or still believes, in God; it's even possible he regularly repents of sin. But his actions betray his true god, an idol that has transfixed humanity from time immaterial: Wealth.

Greed fueled Bishop Ntabazi and many others to swindle their fellow Ugandans for what little they had. One such Ugandan is Daniel Leinhardt.

In mid-2016, Leinhardt was spending his days raising chickens and helping his father work long, hard hours harvesting corn. Their goal was to save enough money to open a store that sold maize and its numerous byproducts, providing a business to sustain the family.

Daniel's financial plans changed, however, when word of OneCoin began to spread throughout the community. Curious, Daniel attended a seminar and was immediately taken by the incredible opportunity that the new cryptocurrency promised.

"If I was to sell my house," he explains in an exclusive interview for this book, "I believed it didn't matter, because in six months I would be able to buy a mansion."

Eager to get in on the new business, Leinhardt returned to his father and told him of this alternate path for the family.

"You are my most educated son," his father told him. "I trust you."

The two traveled to the slick, upscale OneCoin offices in the Ugandan capital of Kampala to hear the presentation. The possibilities seemed like a dream come true.

"It was something I wanted," Leinhardt recalls. "Easy money, no working, no hustling. Just use your smartphone and start to see your money increase every single day."

The family thought and prayed about the matter for three days, then decided to invest. Leinhardt took his father's fifteen million Ugandan shillings, equivalent to about $2,500 USD, and handed it to a OneCoin promoter who assured him he was making the best decision of his life. A day later Daniel returned and offered more cash to deposit, this from his own chicken business that he had otherwise used to pay university fees.

Father and son returned to their lives confident in their investment. "As the price of our OneCoin continued to go up, we would calculate how much money we had—though we could not yet touch it," Daniel shares, his tone heavy with irony. "My father and I started looking for beautiful houses on websites that sold homes. We looked at nice, trendy houses — it was crazy, because at the time you calculate millions of dollars and wonder: Will I spend the money or buy a new farm? It was so hard to realize that our expectations wouldn't happen at all."

For the Leinhardt family, the shine of OneCoin didn't take long to fade. Their investment, their "coins," were inaccessible, always locked behind promises of the coming "exchange." While their money seemed to be growing, it never got any closer to their pockets.

Then in 2017, Dr. Ruja disappeared. Whispers of fraud became shouts, and soon the word reached Ugandan neighborhoods. Daniel and his family were crushed.

"My father struggles to trust me and there are times when the burden comes back," Daniel says, speaking of how things are today with his father. "I can never tell if [he] is angry at me, or just upset in general, because I was the one who brought our family to OneCoin."

Understandably, Daniel's father is hopeful that his son will right past wrongs by finding riches and success. Given the number of scams wreaking havoc on under-resourced Ugandans, and the lack of consistent financial oversight from the government, the odds remain high that more scams like OneCoin will be successful. [3]

This exacerbates an already rampant poverty trap in these countries. When governments don't provide essential protections and infrastructure to balance the playing field, many will become desperate for any opportunity that comes their way. This gives enterprises like OneCoin the chance to pass themselves off as a legitimate opportunity for those who can't count on their country's economy or law enforcement to protect them.

There are some lights at the end of Daniel's tunnel. In early 2022, high-ranking OneCoin promoter Pastor John Mwambusya was arrested by Ugandan authorities for defrauding thousands of victims. A key member of the multi-level pyramid, Mwambusya developed a reputation for leading his congregants in chants of "OneCoin, OneLife," just as Bishop Fred Ntabazi had. He was also connected to the leadership of OneCoin's DealShaker platform and regularly directed people to demonstrate their faith by purchasing goods from the site. We'll discuss DealShaker and its dubious nature momentarily.

Pastor John could very well have gotten away with his crimes against the Ugandan people for even longer; however, Daniel reported him again and again to the Ugandan financial investigation authority. After he started submitting inquiries, Daniel heard nothing from the government for months. But consequences came for Mwambusya in February of 2022, a shocking relief to a population used to bureaucrats who frequently turn a blind eye to these kinds of schemes. [4]

Yet it's just a drop in the bucket of justice. The Leinhardts, like thousands of other Ugandans, still don't have their money. Daniel had to drop out of university and focus on raising hens, breeding them, and selling the eggs. He now dedicates much of his attention to a YouTube channel devoted to exposing fraud and bringing its perpetrators to justice. [5]

Don't Worry, It's *Halal*

OneCoin's devastating Ponzi scheme targeted poor nations like those landlocked in Central Africa; it also sought out isolated, marginalized groups in wealthier nations.

When OneCoin arrived in Great Britain, it ensnared more than just working class victims like Jennifer McAdam, and zeroed in on one group in particular: Muslims. The majority of Muslims live in predominantly Islamic nations. OneCoin preferred to steal from populations living *outside* these heavily regulated countries, targeting communities on the fringes of society. These believers tend to live in tightly-knit circles and eagerly seek ways to improve their lives. It was the perfect mark for the OneCoin MLM formula. Muslims, however, were an even more ideal target. Under Muslim law, charging or earning interest is known as *riba*, or usury, and constitutes an unjust act. For this reason, modern Islamists often struggle to find investments that are permitted under *Sharia* law. Therefore investing in assets that gain value in and of themselves, such as real estate, gold, or a business, is completely permissible, or *halal*. To assure devotees of the world's second-largest religion that it was compliant with Muslim law, OneCoin published a certificate of compliance from a center of Islamic banking and economics in Pakistan that purported OneCoin to be both *halal* and a wise investment for its followers worldwide.

The response was immediate and powerful. Thousands of Muslims, many of them living in England, shipped their savings and legacies off to OneCoin's coffers, eager to make a sound financial decision that was pleasing in the sight of Allah. Due to the close-knit nature of Muslims living in a secular nation, these British citizens commonly told their family members, neighbors, and fellow faithful about the new *Shariah*-compliant investment.

Yet the banking center never published such a certificate. The document was a crude forgery, and after receiving word that such a document was circulating online, the Al-Huda Center for Islamic Banking and Investment published a press release declaring that it had *not* made any such assurances about the legality and fiduciary integrity of OneCoin, nor would it ever do so. [6]

Muslim communities were devastated.[7]

When they pressed OneCoin to refund their investments, or—better yet—allow people to exchange OneCoin for fiat currency, the leadership of the company released one of its typical announcements. Investors should remain patient, they said. Developers were hard at work creating a new financial reality through a cutting edge blockchain that was going to transform finance as they knew it. Members would be able to use their coins soon.

This was all a lie.

When members of the OneLife Network pushed for the chance to use their coins to buy something, *anything*, they were referred to the network's online sales platform, Deal-Shaker.

OneCoin relied on DealShaker to deflect criticism in its numerous press releases, primarily when rebutting the claims of BBC podcaster Jamie Bartlett. *There is nothing amiss*, OneCoin's publicist seemed to be saying. *DealShaker is here, so spend your coins at will!*

Yet one would be hard-pressed to find anything of value on DealShaker. Comprised of random, overpriced products, DealShaker listings suggested something of a suspicious eBay-Craigslist hybrid. The photography and written postings did little to reassure buyers that these were anything more than stolen or poorly imitated goods. Even if one could purchase an assortment of random crap on the site, it couldn't be transformed into real, usable money that people needed to buy houses, shop for groceries, or fill their gas tanks. To turn around and sell the DealShaker items would almost never yield a profit, given the prices, which were usually a combination of fiat currency and

OneCoins. It was just another arm of the scam, another way to pull money away from victims. [8]

Tentacles of a Monster

"I want to transform the lives of unbanked people."

At Wembley, Dr. Ruja repeatedly uses a term that creates an aura of charity: *Unbanked people*. The idea that the system has left people behind is not new. It's a common refrain for many world-changers, legitimate and otherwise. [9]

But with Ignatova, the teeth of the wolf can be seen peeking out from under the disguise. When she claims that OneCoin will enable the unbanked to share the financial prosperity of others, she plays to the common sympathy in every human heart. *How generous of her!* the audience is led to think. But the "unbanked" were really Ignatova and Greenwood's most vulnerable marks, the "least of these" who had the fewest defenses against their elaborate ruse. No one was too poor or pitiable to be spared the scam.

The OneCoin Ponzi scheme was one of the most widespread scams to ever befall the human race. One is reminded of the black-and-white, anti-communist newsreels of the 1950s depicting the Soviet Union as a giant octopus with its tentacles encircling the globe. OneCoin was the realization of that propagandist vision of world domination. Like cryptocurrency itself, OneCoin had no boundaries. The crypto con defrauded many wealthy investors including Igor Alberts, perhaps OneCoin's most successful promoter, who lost millions after buying thousands of fake coins in hopes of becoming the richest man on Earth. But these stories are rare and hardly garner much sympathy. While OneCoin was happy to steal from the rich, it stole even more from the poor. To Dr. Ruja Ignatova, Daniel Leinhardst's $2,500 USD was nothing, a single night of fine dining in Sofia. She took it anyway.

In all, the scam hit nearly 175 countries. Promoters in Italy have been fined. India arrested numerous promoters who carried on the lie long after it was found out. Chinese law enforcement recently prosecuted ninety-eight OneCoin promoters for fraud, and reports estimate that nearly $2 billion USD was poached from vulnerable citizens. Testimonies from the infamously strict surveillance state are rare, but the aggression from the government demonstrates just how serious concerns were at the top of the world's second-most populous country. [10]

The OneCoin monster spread its tentacles far and wide, vilifying millions with a golden grin. Yet its incredible expansion exposed cracks in the system that allowed investigators and skeptics to gain ground. Within a few years, there was enough pressure to force Dr. Ruja into hiding. Unfortunately for many like Jen McAdam, Daniel Leinhardt, and millions more, these law enforcement agents would be too late.

The most remarkable evil of OneCoin is the way it weaponized people's culture, faith, and virtues against those same individuals. When examining a scam of this scale, it can be easy to blame the victims for not getting wise to the scheme earlier. And while there are certainly cases where this may be applicable, one must reckon with the dreadful efficiency of the OneCoin machine. It moved swiftly and aggressively, preying on FOMO and compassion in order to extract as much wealth as possible.

OneCoin blatantly and shamelessly used religion to lie, cheat, and steal from its victims. The falsified *halal* certificate probably took an office employee thirty minutes to fabricate and post online, yet it successfully duped tens of thousands of trusting Muslims. Pastor John shamelessly pushed his Ugandan followers toward DealShaker, likely because he reaped immense profits from purchases on the shady platform. And Bishop Fred Ntabazi devoted days of his life to running One Life International Ministries, a "church" that was less about the Gospel of Jesus Christ than it was the gospel of easy gold.

It's ironic that Ntabazi's church gathered on the fifth floor of the Padre Pio Building in Kampala, Uganda. Padre Pio lived in the early Twentieth Century, surviving two world wars as he tried to spread the love of Jesus to citizens of Europe. Yet as he grew older, he fell into cynicism and despair. According to his biographer, Pio once cried out, "Can't you see the world is on fire?"

For those who trusted OneCoin, the world is on fire. They come from communities with few resources. They gathered what little they had and handed it to a pack of wolves, believing lies that were told with gusto and zeal.

This is why fraud can be so hard to detect. How can one see the world burning when the shine of gold is in our eyes?

Protecting oneself from scams like OneCoin isn't easy, especially when one's country doesn't provide adequate defenses against fraud.

But by exploring the history of OneCoin, similar frauds, and the source of Ponzi schemes, we stand to learn important lessons about the nature of scams that can be turned into an advantage. With knowledge and some savvy, we can mount a stand against these forces of deception.

For without these preventive measures, we stand alone in plain sight, an unwitting feast for the wolves while the flames consume the world around us.

Part 2 - The Con and the Lie: Detecting the Machinery of Fraud

4

Weaponizing Hope

By all accounts, it was a brisk, overcast afternoon in 1903 when the S. S. *Vancouver* chugged into Boston Harbor, its stacks belching thick black clouds of coal-fired smoke. A similar sheen of brown-gray smog hovered over the city, the air choked with exhaust from dozens of factories.

The vessel lowered its ramps and a thin, handsome Italian man strode over the shuddering dock. His coat barely kept the Atlantic winds at bay as he stepped on American soil for the first time, his face boldly set on the New World. Before him was a land of opportunity. He only had $2.50 in his pocket, the rest gambled away after the long journey. However, as he later declared, he had a million dollars in his heart. Within a few days, the man had secured employment as a dishwasher and was spending his free time learning English.

Many of his fellow Italian immigrants changed their surnames, wishing to blend in with the nomenclature of their new culture. But not this man. He had befouled his family name once already after flunking out of university, and this was his opportunity to bring it back.

For the next few years, the man worked hard, mastered the new language, and rose in ranks to become a server and cashier at a restaurant. He did encounter one problem, though: He was fired after customers complained that he was short-changing them and pocketing the difference. The man denied it, of course. It was just a big misunderstanding.

Charles Ponzi swore he'd never steal from anyone.[1]

160 Million Coupons

The name "Ponzi" is infamous today, but few understand exactly what he did and why his name is now synonymous with a particular kind of scam. The details of Ponzi's crimes are strikingly similar to those of Dr. Ruja Ignatova, as are the psychological conditions that allowed so many people to be duped by a con artist.

After several years of job-hopping across the United States and Canada, Ponzi settled outside Boston and cooked up a scheme that is all-too familiar, even if he trafficked a product that isn't well known today. He began his business by purchasing International Reply Coupons, IRCs, that senders would often include in their letters as a courtesy to the recipient. Ponzi found a hole in the system that would allow him to purchase the coupons at a cheap rate in Italy and then resell them in America at a considerable profit. Ponzi elected to exploit this completely legal loophole and began enjoying a comfortable living for himself.

Unfortunately, this level of success wasn't enough for him. Inside this man was an itch to earn more money than he could possibly imagine, to push the boundaries of what he could acquire even if it meant utilizing devious means. To that end, Ponzi began promoting his IRC business as an investment opportunity. Sending teams of recruiters across the United States, Ponzi promised that money entrusted to his coupon company would deliver record-breaking returns of 50% or better and make investors wildly rich. With gold in their eyes, people everywhere sent their money Ponzi's way, believing it would eventually yield a massive payout.

Ponzi, of course, pocketed most of the income. He didn't even bother to move IRCs anymore, and had his team fabricate receipts to send back to investors. He was smart enough to reserve a pile of cash to pay his staff, and to fund requests from investors who wanted to cash out of the business. Yet few customers ever made such requests, as Ponzi's elaborate ruse convinced them that the longer the money stayed in the system, the greater the returns would be. The falsified receipts delivered unbelievable reports of growth and success, placating the vast majority of Ponzi's victims to let their financial savior do his work unbothered.

Throughout the early stretches of Ponzi's business, press coverage was generally favorable. These glowing reviews led even more hardworking people to take out loans, mortgage their homes, and withdraw their life savings so that Charles Ponzi could work his magic. In a way, the press had little choice but to print glowing reports about the flamboyant businessman. Libel laws of the day were unfavorable to journalists making allegations, allowing men like Ponzi to sue anyone who criticized him and couldn't provide 100% proof to back their claims. When a pesky reporter for *The Boston Post* began asking questions about Ponzi's ludicrous profits, he took the paper to court and forced it to back down.

But the *Post* wasn't done with Ponzi. Without going to print, the staff began taking a hard look at the scheme's reported numbers, then spoke to the United States Postal Service. According to the USPS, there were roughly 27,000 International Reply Coupons in circulation worldwide at that time. With even the most generous calculations, this was far too small a number in order for Ponzi to be earning such fantastic returns. To deliver the percentages he was claiming, Ponzi would have needed a staggering 160 *million* coupons to be in circulation. The numbers were impossible, and the promised returns absurd.

In 1920, *The Post* decided to strike back. Clarence Barron, the eventual founder of the respected financial magazine *Barron's*, believed Ponzi to be a liar based on the profits alone. He launched an investigation and published a series of articles in the *Post* that put the heat on Ponzi, who immediately took a very familiar step. Hiring his own writers, he attempted to trash critics through positively-spun newspaper reports. If his plan had gone off, perhaps history would regard Clarence Barron as just another "Hater."

But the plan didn't work. His chosen PR man, William McMasters, refused to lie for him, and instead set the fraudster's reputation ablaze in the press. Ponzi's crimes quickly came to light when law enforcement raided his office and found no postal coupons, proving instantly that the entire enterprise was a ruse. They did, however, find the false investment reports that Ponzi had been sending out to his victims.

Within months, Charles Ponzi was in prison for his crimes. His quest to redeem his family name had backfired, and now it is known for all the wrong reasons. [2]

Sell Nothing, Make a Fortune

The similarities between Ponzi's IRC scam and OneCoin are immediately striking. Just as there were never any coupons in 1920, there were never any coins in 2016. There was never a real exchange where the coins could be used. Even the educational materials that constituted the bulk of the "packages" were crudely copied from Wikipedia and other easily-discovered sources. Ponzi worked the same angle, selling profits from coupons that didn't exist by printing bogus reports and sending them to his investors. [3]

OneCoin emulated this process with Twenty-First Century technology, deploying software that updated the "value" or "price" of an investor's coins based on a predetermined formula. According to the United States Department of Justice, Dr. Ruja Ignatova described exactly how the con would work in a 2015 email to Greenwood: "We can manipulate the exchange by simulating some volatility and intraday pricing."

Then, in a separate communication from the same year, she wrote, "[A]lways close on a high price at end of day, open day with high price, build confidence - better *manipulation* so they are happy," [*emphasis added*]. [4]

Just as Ponzi created fictitious profit reports and shipped them across the country, Ignatova used a computer program to generate fictitious coins that seemed to change in value throughout the day as a normal stock, commodity, or cryptocurrency would. When investors logged into their OneLife accounts to view the value of their mined coins, what they saw wasn't the product of real trades or fluctuations in the marketplace. Instead, OneCoin's victims were treated to a curated illusion, a cryptocurrency-themed online experience. They paid for the fantasy of being crypto investors and were treated to a show by an algorithm that simulated price volatility. Yet somehow the prices never ended lower than before. According to the same DOJ report, "The purported price of OneCoins never decreased in value." [5]

This is the first key takeaway that can bolster our defenses against future scams. In a real market, prices don't just go up; they also go down, and for a time stay down. While they tend to recover, sometimes marvelously, they almost never do so by market close, and never day-after-day.

Asset values are always affected by widespread events as well. Economic recessions, sell-offs, scandals, negative earnings reports: These tend to impact every sector of the global marketplace. But characters like Ponzi and Ignatova somehow created products that never lost value, even in the worst of times.

If this type of deceitful strategy sounds familiar, it's probably because you remember another renowned financial crook: Bernie Madoff. When it comes to selling nothing and making a fortune, no one did it as well as him.

Bernie Madoff was born in Brooklyn and spent most of his life enamored with the world of finance. He traded penny stocks in the 1960s and worked on the fringes of Wall Street, possibly contributing to the chip on his shoulder about his place in the ecosystem of big money. When his firm finally blossomed into a respected investment company, Madoff reportedly earned over $100 million a year.[6]

But sometime in the early 1990s, Madoff set up a second business, a secretive investment advisory service. Operating out of a separate floor from his primary, public-facing business, the investment advisory service was exclusive, secretive, and highly illegal. Claiming to be choosing high-yield funds for his investors, Madoff created customized reports with falsified trades, often using the previous day's newspaper as a guide. The firm seemed to create a perfect world of investing. To Madoff's investors the yields looked like the work of a genius. While every other fund ebbed and flowed with the market, Madoff's always came out ahead.

This caught the eye of investigative journalists. In a moment of irony, a writer for *Barron's* began investigating Madoff's background. Like Ponzi, Madoff went on the offensive. He crafted elaborate excuses and fictional documents to appease the SEC regulators. He told his own version of the story in the press and played the victim. All the while, billions of dollars flowed into Bernie Madoff's 17th floor offices, enriching him and his allies.

Madoff was able to successfully weather years of questions, criticism, and regulation. He couldn't, however, survive the financial crisis of 2007 and 2008. When the markets crashed, Madoff's investors began to cash out. There wasn't any money to give them. Like Ponzi, Madoff had been pocketing the deposits, keeping only a small reserve in place for minimal withdrawals. When requests for hundreds of millions came in, the money simply wasn't there. Worse, Madoff's imaginary trades led his investors to believe that over $60 billion in assets were available. There was no way to keep up the ruse any longer.

Madoff accepted defeat and turned himself in. In depositions he confessed to every aspect of the scheme and pleaded guilty to his decades-long criminal operation. In 2021, Bernie Madoff died at the age of 82 as he served his 150 year sentence. [7]

As with Ponzi and Ignatova, there were no actual goods being sold. No trades, no returns, and no profits. And especially like OneCoin, Madoff's investment firm was treated like a special club, an exclusive loophole in the economic world that would change the lives of a lucky few. Madoff actually turned some investors away if he felt he couldn't properly manipulate them, heightening the allure of his achievements and making investors want to give him their money more than ever. Once again, the power of FOMO conquers all.

Somehow these three individuals—Ponzi, Madoff, and Ignatova—were able to erect stunning business enterprises around a whole lot of nothing and defraud their victims for millions and billions.

How did they do that? And how can we escape the next version of the same scheme that comes our way?

Too Good to Be True?

It's easy to look back on this trio of hoaxes and mutter, "If it's too good to be true, it probably is." Hindsight makes geniuses of everyone.

Yet thousands fell for these rackets, and many of these victims were of considerable intelligence and common sense.

Why couldn't they see the truth?

While these three scams span a century of history and each peddled a unique product, they share a common thread. In a previous chapter we explored the phenomenon of crypto FOMO, a very real and observable phenomenon that caused many people to abandon logic in their decision-making. But this fear of missing out isn't exclusive to cryptocurrency. It is universal, a widespread human emotion that has endured over all generations. The fear has nothing to do with crypto, stocks, or mail coupons. Rather, it has everything to do with easy money.

Aside from a few enlightened monks, there are few people on Earth who wouldn't enjoy an easy payday. The vast majority of people work incredibly hard and make little to show for it. A select, lucky few win the lottery of life and are born to wealthy parents, possess innate brilliance, or capitalize on a market trend at exactly the right time.

Most of us do not.

People want to be lucky. Just look at the vast number of casinos throughout the world. Inside of each are hundreds of human beings with a burning desire to be special, to be a "chosen one" like the heroes of *Harry Potter*, *Star Wars*, or any other epic tale.

But with over seven billion people on the planet, it's hard to top the pile in every respect, and many are dissatisfied with the hand life has dealt them. They are eager to be the lucky ones and show up at the right time and in the right place. This is human nature. It is not a good or evil, at least as much as this author will judge. But it is innately human to long for a place of importance and substance on the stage of life, and Ponzi schemes are designed to exploit this very instinct.

It's not entirely foolish to hope for this kind of fortune; people do occasionally find it. Not every rich person started that way. For some, the universe rolls the dice and the results are favorable. For many, they are not.

But, we are tempted to think, *they could be!*

Even though logic, common sense, and cynicism scream otherwise, we still want to believe something that is "too good to be true" *actually is true*. It's the stuff of every heroic tale from Disney to Marvel to the Bible. Good triumphs over evil. Someone who sacrifices is resurrected. The good guys win in the end.

And who plays the "good guy" in the narrative of our own lives other than ourselves? Why can't I be the lucky one, we often ask. Haven't I worked hard all my life? Shouldn't I be able to provide extravagant luxuries for my family?

Why not *me*?

Just like her fraudulent forebears, Dr. Ruja Ignatova knew exactly what she was doing when she designed OneCoin to be a blatant scam. In 2014, the get-lucky-and-rich-overnight flavor of the week was cryptocurrency, and thanks to her experience at BigCoin, Ignatova knew how to assemble a passable facade around her invisible product. She knew the jargon and was able to present it in a flashy, spectacular package. Paired with Greenwood and his knowledge of multi-level marketing, she had the perfect pitch to overwhelm her victims' common sense and skepticism. [8]

They had an answer to practically every question.

How could OneCoin make such unbelievable returns?

We are doing cryptocurrency better than BitCoin.

How is OneCoin better than BitCoin?

We have a revolutionary blockchain that provides safe, secure, and fast transactions.

Can I exchange my OneCoin for other money or goods?

Yes, on DealShaker! Soon it will be accepted everywhere, once the haters and Big Banks stop slowing us down.

Another important takeaway from this brief look at the history of Ponzi schemes is to note a common, timeless thread: Impossible financial promises.

One may not be able to fully research and understand International Return Coupons, Wall Street investments, or cryptocurrency. However, one *can* research the current price, laws, and regulations around almost any product. One can read articles, reports, and investigative journalism about it. And thanks to modern technology, one can read reviews and eye-witness accounts of the product, the sales experience, and its results.

We don't need to be experts on whatever product-of-the-month is being peddled. We do, however, need to be experts on our own hearts, and whether they are being manipulated to abandon logic and reason.

Are the expected financial returns historically proven?

Is there adequate regulation to provide oversight?

When gold-tongued promises begin to rain down, guarantees of wildly outlandish sales, financial returns, or non-stop successes, then our fraud radar needs to start flashing right away. This is one of the clearest signs that we are being targeted by a scammer. When the emotional heat is turned up, the chances increase that we are either being scammed or legally ripped off.

As we've seen, Ignatova and her forebears were happy to take advantage of the uneducated, marginalized, impoverished, and disenfranchised. The scammer moves toward the vulnerable and exploits those who know enough to invest but too little to scrutinize. The pitch is carefully crafted with strong, emotional language that inflames the heart and overwhelms the head. Before long, buyers aren't thinking through their purchase, but *feeling* it. [9]

We can't research everything that's out there, but we can take careful stock of what's happening between our ears and inside our chests. If the promises seem too good to be true—or are made with heady jargon or passionate verbiage—then we must take caution, pump the proverbial brakes, and avoid a hasty decision based on anything but prudent logic.

Is there a chance you might miss out on the latest wave of get-rich-quick opportunities?

Possibly.

But is there a *greater* chance that someone is trying to take your hard-earned money in an elaborate scam or ripoff?

Yes.

We can never truly know why some among us get lucky and others don't. The best advice on that matter is to avoid taking things personally and don't blame your god, the universe, or anything spiritual for it. Sometimes things just don't work out.

But we can avoid being particularly *unlucky* by practicing this advice and avoiding any offers that are *truly* too-good-to-be-true or are made in a manipulative fashion.

In the end, we have a power that the scammers can't take from us: The power to walk away.

5

"THERE IS NO BLOCKCHAIN"

IN OCTOBER OF 2016, BJORN BJERCKE RECEIVED A strange phone call. It came from a recruiter working for a company that preferred not to reveal its name. The company had been running a cryptocurrency for over two years and needed a Chief Operating Officer. More specifically, they needed someone to build a blockchain.

At this, the hairs on Bjercke's neck stood on end.

According to Bjercke's story, as told to Jamie Barlett on *The Missing CryptoQueen* podcast, the fact that this crypto start-up didn't have a blockchain was a huge red flag. Even though the job came with perks like a company car, a house in Sofia, and a six-figure salary, Bjercke passed. [1]

For the average person who doesn't deal in cryptocurrency terminology, this may not seem like a big deal. "Just build them a blockchain," one might say. This naivete about crypto technology is one of the many reasons OneCoin was so successful. It peddled a product in a confusing market and trusted that people wouldn't look into the finer details.

But a blockchain is essential to cryptocurrency in the same way that houses are essential to real estate. To sell a cryptocurrency without a blockchain is to take payments on houses that don't exist, and never will.

If that's the case, how did OneCoin sell billions worth of currency that was never really there?

And how can we avoid falling victim to similar scams when they are eventually unleashed on the world?

"Switching On the Blockchain"

Earlier that year, Dr. Ruja Ignatova delivered her sweeping speech to the crowd at Wembley Arena. Roughly half an hour into her talk, Ignatova declared, "We will be switching on the new blockchain. OneCoin will officially become the #1 cryptocurrency globally!"

Once the thunderous applause died down, she went into further detail about how OneCoin's blockchain would revolutionize cryptocurrency: "Our blockchain can do more transactions than Visa and Mastercard put together. In October, we will retire the old blockchain and launch a new, more powerful blockchain than before."

This won Iganatova even more raucous applause. The old was being replaced, and the new was going to change the world. [2]

Except that's not how blockchain works.

A real blockchain cannot be switched off. A true blockchain underpinning a real cryptocurrency is decentralized, shared across thousands of devices on a network. If one machine turns off, the blockchain remains, shared amongst the numerous other machines. This is why one computer can't delete all the BitCoin in the world, because BitCoin isn't powered by a single source.

For Bjercke, OneCoin's loose language with crypto terminology was a massive concern. It alerted him to more than just incompetence; it screamed fraud.

For the rest of us who aren't experts in digital, decentralized currencies, these words probably don't ring alarm bells, and it didn't concern the vast majority of OneCoin's investors. The techy-jargon fit their expectations. When they imagined "switching on the blockchain," they probably equated it to an operative service update, like something one might install on their smartphone.

Fraudulent operations depend on the ignorance of their victims. Scammers craft messages that contain just enough content vocabulary to sound authentic, and whenever marks begin to question, the scammer pivots toward fear and intimidation.

The reality is OneCoin never had a blockchain. It's possible that Ignatova and Greenwood didn't even know how blockchain works, given the errors in the slideshow that 2016 night in Wembley:

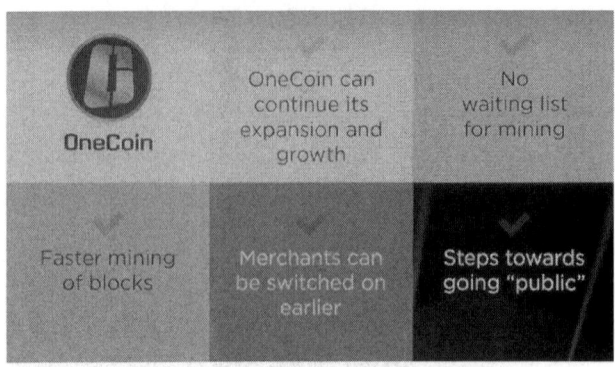

	OneCoin can continue its expansion and growth	No waiting list for mining
OneCoin		
Faster mining of blocks	Merchants can be switched on earlier	Steps towards going "public"

Ignatova, Dr. Ruja and One Coin. "The Blockchain," YouTube, 11 July 2016. https://www.youtube.com/watch?v=638 _Jpp2Rq8&t=1980s&ab_channel=OneCoin

The bottom left tile reads "Faster mining of blocks," something that seems attractive at first glance. Yet blocks are not mined in cryptocurrency. Coins are mined by the formation of blocks. This seemingly minute detail is actually quite the bombshell as we shall soon see.

The top-center line is a fraught matter as well, if one knows the key differences between a cryptocurrency and other investment products. For OneCoin to continue its "expansion and growth" sounds like a great thing, which is true for practically any other company.

But for currency, expansion means something different: Access to trade. This never happened for OneCoin.

Instead, Ignatova's idea of "expansion and growth" appeared minutes later in the speech when she makes a seemingly wonderful proclamation: "For people who supported us through Phase 1, because we're moving into a huge Phase 2 now, whatever coins you have on your account or in the mining, ...what we will do as a company is double the coins on your account." [3]

The response was immediate: The crowd went nuts. People who were already convinced that OneCoin was going to make them wealthy suddenly believed that they had just *doubled* their riches. To anyone fully grafted into Dr. Ruja's cult, this was like being told that God was going to return in just a few short days.

Yet the economics of this make no sense. Doubling production or the capability of a supply chain makes total sense when the item of value is a good or service. Tech companies do this all the time in the lead-up to the holidays, hoping to avoid shortages in stock.

However, this isn't how currency works. To double the amount of currency in a marketplace doesn't make it twice as valuable. It actually has the *reverse* effect. In the same way that printing money causes inflation in a traditional economy, doubling digital currency will only decrease the value of each coin in the system.

Worse, Ignatova unwittingly reveals that she has the ability to add coins to the OneCoin ecosystem at will, something that defies the very nature of cryptocurrency and blockchain technology. [4]

Perhaps this can all be chalked up to careless semantic error. Yet it betrays the overall lack of understanding of how cryptocurrency—or even traditional fiat currency—works. Ignatova and her partners were able to weave a convincing web for many of their supporters by deploying the jargon of cryptocurrency. But that same diction led people like Bjerke to start asking questions and researching OneCoin, eventually revealing just how illegitimate the purported cryptocurrency was.

So just how does cryptocurrency work? Does it really matter in this case?

The answer is a resounding 'Yes,' and the reasons why stand to help us in our quest to avoid becoming victims ourselves.

Establishing Trust

Why is money worth anything?

Perhaps you've paused to wonder how a piece of paper can be worth only one dollar, euro, pound, or shilling, while another is worth a hundred. Why, you might ask, do some currencies gain value while others lose it? Why is the dollar 'up' and the euro 'down'?

These questions are yet another reason Dr. Ruja's con worked so spectacularly. Economics is an incredibly complicated subject, made infinitely more convoluted by the behavior of actual people in actual markets. Currencies rise and fall thanks to myriad individual factors, too many to cover here. However, it almost always has to do with the currency's *perceived* value, and perceived value is based on trust.

Practically anything can be currency. Ancient peoples used cowries, lumps of silver, metal coins, gold and other precious metals, and even patches of leather. But why were these things themselves considered valuable? Some are beautiful and can be fashioned into jewelry, but most are dull, heavy, and undesirable for adornment. Why then would someone accept a handful of cowries for a pig, a house, or even a daughter's hand in marriage? And why not accept other things that are in abundance, like rocks, leaves, or sand?

For something to have value, it must possess two qualities: Scarcity and resilience.

First, scarcity means that there is an end to its supply. When something is limited, it has the potential to be valuable. Things with practically unlimited quantity, however, are easily obtained and lack the same sense of value. This is why sand isn't used as currency. There's so much of it that no one would ever make sacrifices to acquire it.

Metals like copper, platinum, silver, gold, aluminum, and tin, however, *are* scarce. They require effort to dig out of the ground, refine, and process. People regularly make sacrifices to get their hands on these materials because acquiring them isn't as easy as scooping a bucket of sand from the beach.

These metals can also be applied to a wide variety of uses and retain their value. This is the second quality: Resilience. Currency must be able to weather the storm of repeated use and abuse. We've all come across a rather battered note of currency in our lives, and while paper money will get creased, torn, and dog-earred to no end, these pieces of paper are surprisingly resilient. This is why things like leaves and grass will never work as currency.

To treat something as a currency, it must be a resilient item that is in limited supply. One wants to have enough of it to provide for an entire society and allow for transactions with a wide range of price exchanges. One also doesn't want to have so much of it that nobody will sacrifice—work and/or save—for it.

This is the key to currency. People have to be able to trust in its value. And how do they demonstrate that trust? By sacrificing in order to acquire it.

So if cryptocurrency is digital, how does it establish trust with its users? What's to stop someone from copying-and-pasting their BitCoins a thousand times and spending them as if they are limitless grains of sand?

In the late 1990s, computer programmer Sean Parker gained infamy by creating Napster, an online file-sharing server that allowed users to upload, share, and then download practically any digital file. Before long Parker was facing lawsuits from several recording artists, most memorably Metallica, for enabling the piracy of intellectual property. This may come to mind when wondering how cryptocurrency works. Wouldn't digital currency encounter the same financial issues that photos, music, and movies did when they went online?

There's a reason BitCoin has lasted over a decade and a half on the world stage. Creator Satoshi Nakamoto understood the principles of currency and wanted to make a new one with unique advantages. Digital currency, at least as Nakamoto envisioned it, is nationless. Its value doesn't fluctuate just because a president is overthrown in a coup or because its treasury department foolishly inflates the currency's value into the gutter, as Germany did pre-World War II.

But the problem of "double-spending" was at the forefront of Nakamoto's design. Double-spending is exactly what it sounds like: Spending the same piece of currency twice.

So how exactly did Nakamoto prevent double-spending with his digital currency, therefore establishing sufficient trust to make BitCoin a legitimate item with tangible value?

He created the blockchain. [5]

The blockchain prevents double-spending *and* guarantees that there will be a limited number of BitCoins in circulation. In the simplest terms, the blockchain is a chain of transactions. Whenever a unit of BitCoin is exchanged, it is anonymously recorded into this online record. It is encrypted and encoded in such a way that it cannot be changed. If a single device on the network attempts to change it, all the others will quickly overrule the change. The process of verifying these transactions is also the one that mints new "coins," awarding them to the decentralized user who successfully verifies the most transactions in a block.

Thanks to this clever technological maneuver, cryptocurrency can be both scarce and resilient, meaning it can be (and is) used as an item of value.

This is why Bjorne Bjercke didn't take the job with OneCoin. If this cryptocurrency start-up had been selling coins for two years but didn't have a blockchain, it could only mean one thing: The "coins" weren't actual cryptocurrency and were inherently worthless. There was no tracking, verification, or prevention of double-spending. Instead, the company had been writing its buyers IOUs with no intention of ever paying them. It was as if Ignatova had sold pieces of paper with random numbers written on them, hired someone, then said, "Make these papers worth the numbers I wrote on them." It's simply absurd because it defies how currency works. The investors just didn't know it.

This is why Ignatova's weaponizing of crypto FOMO was so devilishly effective. It convinced investors to turn off their skepticism about cryptocurrency and trust the leader of the movement. Even one of OneCoin's senior executives, Ed Ludbrook, once boasted, "You don't have to understand about how the blockchain… works. I have a background in economics and engineering and all sorts of stuff, and I don't have anything to do with it. I just trust Ruja. If people ask me very technical questions, I go, 'I don't know, I trust Dr. Ruja,' and she's never let me down." [6]

OneCoin buyers didn't seem to understand blockchain either, but they definitely considered Dr. Ruja a trustworthy entrepreneur who would never do them wrong. Their hope was in her alone.

How to Sniff Out a Scam

Tempting as it may be, hindsight and schadenfreude won't help us prepare for the next convoluted scam. Ignatova and Greenwood were clever to choose a cryptocurrency for their con, given its obscurity in mainstream communities and circles. For years, OneCoin operated without a real blockchain and didn't seem too concerned about it, as no one of significant stature asked the right questions.

Yet in late 2016, something scared OneCoin's corporate headquarters into trying to build a blockchain, leading them to reach out to Bjorne Bjerke. The scam was growing more rapidly than ever, and the international scrutiny was getting intense. Ignatova couldn't rely on keeping all her victims ignorant of the lack of a legitimate blockchain.

Yet the damage was done. No self-respecting developer was going to work with OneCoin without telling the press. And despite its efforts to keep itself anonymous, OneCoin was about to be exposed. Bjercke refused to let the fraud continue unchecked and was one of the first to blow the whistle. [7]

So the question remains: How could OneCoin's investors have known it was all a lie? How can we learn these lessons without suffering the same injustices?

Ignatova and Greenwood worked hard to cover their tracks. They weren't above forging false documents from a theocratic government, as with the *halal* certification. They didn't consider it excessive to invade Uganda and victimize its poor, under-resourced population. And they always had an answer for the haters, full-throated rebuttals that excoriated critics of their beloved deliverer.

What, then, could people do to defend themselves?

Yes, they could have walked away, but this revisionist criticism doesn't account for all the reasons *not* to walk away. The presentations were slick and professional. According to Jen McAdam, the webinar presentation for OneCoin was filled with reasons to invest. She was wowed not only by the seeming technical knowhow of the presenters, but by the "OneCoin family," and how "[they used] very family-oriented words."

Ruja's credentials also sold McAdam. The Glasgow resident decided to perform her own background check and searched for information about Dr. Ruja. What she found was overwhelmingly positive. Specifically, she found a video of Ignatova speaking at a conference for *The Economist*.

"That did it for me," she told Jamie Bartlett. [8]

Ignatova's lecture at *The Economist* Forum is rather subdued compared to OneCoin's more bombastic events. She delivers her speech in the same tone and style as she would during a TED Talk. She dons the trademark earrings and gown, but lacks the flash and charisma of other speeches. She is, frankly, quite believable.

Rewatching this speech today, it is sometimes shocking to think that Ignatova knew then that everything she was saying was a lie.

Yet she lived the lie with absolute confidence and commitment. When Ignatova speaks, one can't help but feel her passion for revolutionizing money, payments, and global systems to favor the unbanked and financially disadvantaged.

Somehow every bit of it was an elaborate performance. The crypto queen never broke character, even when facing tough questions from powerful bank executives, media personalities, promoters of rival cryptocurrency, and skeptical investors. In public, Ignatova was unshakeable in her delivery of the OneCoin narrative. [9]

If this is the face of the scam, and if someone like Jen McAdam conducted research and came away with nothing but assurances that Dr. Ruja was the real deal, how then was she supposed to defend herself? How could she know that everything about Ignatova and OneCoin was the most elaborate hoax ever conceived?

There are few steps left at this point; yet they remain, and are the last hope we have against those who would defraud us without mercy or remorse. One cannot say whether or not OneCoin's victims should have done more, or even could have. But for the purposes of this discussion, these are the few remaining tools at the public's disposal when faced with something that might be a scam.

1. Ask: "Who are the established experts in this field?"

Prior to investing your hard-earned resources, look into the names and faces that make up the established set of experts regarding the product, service, or philosophy you're being sold.

If someone is selling you something "new" or "revolutionary," gather as much information as you can about the ingredients and processes behind the product, then start looking for experts on these specific kinds of items. What have people recently written or said about them? What disagreements currently exist? What does the research and science say about the benefits and risks?

While the people selling this product will claim to be experts, and may argue that you need not investigate further, do so anyway. There is safety in numbers, so the saying goes, and we'd be wise to gather as many voices as possible prior to making a high stakes decision.

2. Observe: "Are the results/responses varied and authentic?"

In an authentic marketplace with real, tangible products, the results *should* be somewhat mixed. Very few products and services are without negative perceptions or reviews. Even the best movies have their haters; even the top-rated restaurants send some diners away dissatisfied.

The same is true with items and ideas hawked by scammers, with one exception: The purported outcomes are always *outlandishly* positive.

Think of Madoff's and Ponzi's unrealistic returns, and how they never flagged with the rest of the economy when it took a dive. Everything in life has a bad day, week, or month. Only cults and scams deal in absolute outcomes.

If you're being told that the PRODUCT is marvelous and always works, while the ESTABLISHMENT PRODUCT is terrible and broken and never works, then there's a good chance someone is trying to angle you into making a rash decision.

3. Ask and Research: "What do I still not know, and need to know, before investing?"

With a general idea of the product and what experts have to say about it, figure out what's left to know before investing. Start asking follow-up questions and researching the information on your own.

With OneCoin, the smoking gun was the lack of an actual blockchain. The only way to have known this would be to thoroughly study and understand how blockchain works.

The following is a matter of personal preference, but one must consider: Is it easier to spend the time investigating and acquiring a serviceable knowledge of blockchain, or easier to regain thousands of lost dollars, pounds, euros, or shillings that have been swindled away?

Every scam will take a different shape. Like the "boggart" creatures of *Harry Potter* lore, scams come to us in forms that are tailored to our vulnerabilities and desires. Our job is to overcome the shine, jargon, polished personal appearances, and appeal to pathos, and then make a reasoned, rational decision.

It's quite possible that one could follow these steps to the letter, approaching an offer with the utmost care and scrutiny, and still fall into the clutches of a scam. Some, like OneCoin, are that damned good at it.

That leaves us with one final option.

4. *Feel: "Is there anything about this that gives off Ponzi, MLM, or cult vibes?"*

Sometimes you have to go with your gut. Despite all the head knowledge one can obtain about Ponzi cons, multi-level marketing schemes, and fraudulent offerings, sometimes it's a funny feeling in our bellies that makes the difference.

It can be any single aspect that sets it off, like an overly zealous "us" vs. "them" mentality. A salesperson who isn't just energetic but urgent. Products that promise miracle results that common sense says aren't truly possible. Vague, meandering answers to questions that should be easy, quick responses. Invitations to join a "family," "team," or "community" that are really just sales networks. A leader who is messianic or absolute in their knowledge, authority, and/or purity.

Perhaps the best advice we can glean from the OneCoin scam is that smooth-talking salespeople with riches on their lips almost *never* have the wellbeing of the buyer in mind. This, too, may sound hurtful to some, as many make their bread by selling reputable products. But when all signs point to a pyramid scheme, and the success is "risk free" or "100% guaranteed," then people should run as fast as they can.

This isn't to suggest that OneCoin's victims "should have known better." It's possible some could have, but there are simply too many victims and villains to paint with such a broad brush. If anything, something must be said about the well-dressed, perfectly-produced art of OneCoin and its ability to convince buyers that they didn't need to know anything about cryptocurrency in order to throw their life savings into it.

When properly resourced, we must research more thoroughly and exhaustively than ever before in this age of international, online business. Our loved ones may be trustworthy in many matters, but they may not understand the intricate workings of cutting-edge technology. We may be struggling to pay the bills, hustling paycheck-to-paycheck, but it is almost never possible to get rich overnight without any hard work and sacrifice.

These schemes prey on trust, and OneCoin went a step further by obfuscating the nature of how trust works when it comes to money and where money gets its value. OneCoin was valuable because Dr. Ruja said it was. Little more needed to be proven.

The Empress Has No BlockChain

To detect the machinery of a con, one must begin with the machinist. For many, Dr. Ruja was a worthy savior, delivering her people from financial slavery. But some saw through the glittering disguise and began to criticize the empress for her lack of even a modest blockchain.

"I have been accused by the so-called community of cryptocurrency," Dr. Ruja remarked with a sneer of derision during her 2016 Wembley address, "'she is violating the philosophy of cryptocurrency.'" [10]

The warning signs were there but difficult to find. Each was accompanied by the "hater" label, further obscuring the truth for people considering investment.

Was this the life-changing opportunity one waits for, led by a revolutionary entrepreneur and business genius?

Or was it as fundamentally broken as its critics claimed, sure to ruin anyone who decided to invest?

Hindsight makes it easy to judge, but the OneCoin machine was incredibly effective at fooling victims into believing it was the real deal. To say that the only option for some was to just say "No" is less an insult to them than it is a compliment to Ignatova and Greenwood for the sinister efficiency of their work. They left most victims with few options, mostly because they chose victims with hardly any options to begin with.

This is perhaps the most gut-wrenching revelation from the OneCoin scam: Victims were always on the margins, weakened by some aspect of their situation. The poor, the elderly, and ethnic minorities are among the most regularly targeted by scammers, a show of the utter remorselessness of this heinous industry. If the machinery of a fraud thrives off the blood of those on the fringes of society, it might behoove people to consider the motives of those who come with gilded promises.

One should ask, Is *this truly for my good?*

Or is it actually designed to make others rich at my expense?

Part 3 - The Hunt for the Queen

6

JUSTICE FOR SOME

D R. RUJA WASN'T A FOOL. SHE KNEW THE CON couldn't last forever.

In a series of texts to Sebastian Greenwood in September 2016, Ignatova revealed her contingency plan as she boarded a flight from Frankfurt to Sofia.

"If sth [sic] happens[, m]y brother knows what to do and will inform you[.]" [1]

Ruja's brother, Konstantin, wasn't captain of the OneCoin ship when it set sail, but he was at the helm as it rammed into an iceberg of international law enforcement. Rumored to keep a signed power of attorney on his person at all times prior to his sister's disappearance, Konstantin Ignatova was handsome, muscular, and heavily tattooed. He made an unlikely leader of the crypto empire started by his gown-wearing, lipstick-daubed sister, but the job fell to him when Ruja fell off the face of the Earth. [2]

The criminal element apparently spread to each limb of the Ignatova family tree, as evidenced by Ruja and her father's corrupt management of the Allgäu factory, and Konstantin was no exception. Through the rest of 2017, 2018, and the start of 2019, Konstantin continued to scam victims out of millions until his reign came to an end in Los Angeles when he stepped off a flight at LAX and found himself surrounded by FBI agents. With his arrest, the OneCoin regime finally collapsed. [3]

The question turned to that of justice. So many scammers abscond with their money into the dark unpunished; others lose their leaders only to spawn new heads and start fresh.

Would the perpetrators of the OneCoin Ponzi actually face justice? Or would they weasel their way out and return to their crooked ways?

And what actually became of Dr. Ruja, the mastermind of it all?

The Net Tightens

It could be said that Dr. Ruja began planning her escape before OneCoin was even founded.

In 2014 Ignatova emailed Greenwood and suggested possible exit strategies. "Take the money and run and blame someone for this," she wrote.

Apparently Ruja was the only one actively putting these pieces in place for an eventual escape. By 2016, she knew she was under investigation thanks to well-placed sources in the Bulgarian government and wiretaps on the phone of another illicit lover and money laundering lawyer, Gilbert Armenta. [4, 5]

JUSTICE FOR SOME 91

Before she vanished without a trace in November of 2017, OneCoin faced constant scrutiny from whistleblowers and financial watchdogs. To calm the stormy waters, Ignatova and Greenwood scheduled a OneCoin event in Lisbon, Portugal, where they promised to ease concerns and discuss plans to open the online exchange and possibly even take OneCoin public.

OneCoin promotor Igor Alberts reflected on this moment with Jamie Barlett: "Dr. Ruja was extremely disciplined. It never happened that she didn't show up for an appointment; she was always on time, not one minute late." [6]

Yet Dr. Ruja didn't appear at the Lisbon conference, a shocking break in her routine of strict punctuality. Greenwood told the faithful that Ruja was on maternity leave, having recently given birth to a daughter, and for a time the troubled masses of OneCoin investors believed it.

Still, some of the higher-ranked members knew something was up. "We saw the desperation on [Konstantin's] face, calling to his sister, and we could not figure it out," Alberts recalled. "Nobody knew why she was not there." [7]

Weeks went by, then months, without Dr. Ruja making any public statements or appearances. Investors wanted to hear from their queen but she was nowhere to be found.

At first the devotees didn't fear that they had been scammed, but that Ruja had been kidnapped by big banks that were threatened by OneCoin's success. The person spreading this rumor was Konstantin. As he took the helm and did all he could to explain away Ruja's absence, Konstaintin also began pushing a popular narrative: The idea that OneCoin was about to go public and launch its global exchange. The dangling carrot had been deployed. [8]

But time was running out for Konstantin, his inherited Ponzi scheme, and his closest advisors. In 2018, Karl Sebastian Greenwood opened the door of his luxurious residence in Thailand to find a team of government officials waiting for him with a warrant in hand. He was placed under arrest and immediately extradited to the United States. For years he seemed to hold out, making no statements or pleas. But in December of 2022, the news broke that Greenwood was facing an array of financial crimes. Charged with three separate counts of fraud, all carrying a maximum sentence of twenty years each, Greenwood plead guilty to all of them.[9]

The man who coupled OneCoin to the fangs of MLM, who referred to his victims as "idiots" and gleefully called his product "trashy coin," had finally been brought to justice.[10]

Loose Ends

Thankfully, Greenwood isn't the only one caught in law enforcement's net. Within a few months, other key leaders began finding themselves in handcuffs.

One of OneCoin's richest lawyers, Mark Scott, enjoyed an illegal windfall to the tune of $50 million while laundering ten times that amount for the company. Later, little over a year after Greenwood's arrest, Konstantin Ignatova arrived in Los Angeles and was taken into custody. It wasn't long before the would-be emperor flipped and promised to tell authorities everything he knew about his sister and her incarcerated partner.[11]

JUSTICE FOR SOME 93

With the arrests of Greenwood and Konstantin Ignatova, the OneCoin scam began to fizzle into a scattered, leaderless hodgepodge of low-level conmen. Most of these figures were former promoters with ambitions of keeping the financial faucets running. Yet this decision ended poorly for many of them.

Argentinian investigators caught up to a slough of ex-promoters and arrested eight of them in December of 2020, including a former radio host who used his platform to push OneCoin investments through his own company. Following a series of raids, law enforcement captured the scammers and put an end to the OneCoin ruse in their nation. [12]

Promoters in other nations have seen their fortunes decline. Italy has arrested a number of criminals related to OneCoin, as has Singapore. The Chinese and Indian governments have responded to reports of OneCoin promoters with swift prosecution.

Perhaps the most grisly response to the fraud occurred in Mexico in June 2020. Two OneCoin promoters vanished and were reportedly kidnapped in a neighborhood within the city of Mazatlan. Two days later police discovered their strangulated bodies in a pair of suitcases that had been dumped in a vacant lot. [13]

After a shocking number of arrests, trials, imprisonments, and murders, the OneCoin regime has largely crumbled. A few of its capos, those who were in on the con and kept it going long after learning the truth, have been brought to justice.

Others, like Dr. Ruja, have not.

Many OneCoin promoters didn't know it was a scam, at least right away. That doesn't mean they weren't complicit. Igor Alberts was the most successful OneCoin promoter in the world, but after Ruja disappeared, Alberts began to worry. He soon jumped ship and his extensive MLM network fled with him, migrating to a new cryptocurrency that is, to this day, considered spurious and possibly another Ponzi. Police in Alberts' home city of Amsterdam have yet to arrest him, lacking any solid evidence linking him to the brains behind these schemes, but they have searched his estate on multiple occasions. Whether or not he knows ahead of time, Alberts seems to keep showing up on fraud's doorstep, eager to profit off spoils from the pyramid.[14]

Dozens more lawyers, businesspeople, and promoters have been incarcerated across the globe. While some still seek to scam people out of their hard-earned money in the name of OneCoin, very few are able to do so.

A question still remains. If so many are behind bars, where do OneCoin's victims stand regarding financial restitution?

In other words, will they ever get their money back?

Getting Away With It

OneCoin victims have been trying to get their $4 billion back for years. Had the company operated in a single country, doing so might have been easy.

But the OneCoin Ponzi spanned the globe and took advantage of myriad loopholes in international finance. It didn't store its stolen goods in a single hoard. Instead,

Dr. Ruja and Greenwood created a nefariously complicated web of interconnected shell companies, trademarks, and LLCs to funnel and hide their earnings. These companies resided in roughly a dozen independent, sovereign nations, each with its own regulating bodies and laws. If you've ever wondered how someone can run a fraudulent Ponzi scheme today and get away with it for so long, perhaps this provides helpful context.

According to court documents filed by attorney Dr. Jonathan Levy, an attorney seeking restitution for victims of the fraud, Ignatova and Greenwood stashed the money in several of these remote island banks. They also bought millions in real estate with the cash, including property in Dubai. Other accounts bearing Dr. Ruja's name are no longer in her control since she left power of attorney documents granting control to influential figures in the oligarchy the rules over the United Arab Emirates. [15]

Lawyers continue to battle over assets with Ruja's name. A listing for a penthouse in London recently revealed that its owner was the missing crypto queen. As for the money in OneCoin accounts in the UAE, entire teams of lawyers are jousting for control, including representatives for Ignatova, Greenwood, one of the sheiks, and victims of the OneCoin scam. Like so many pursuits for justice, matters are in the hands of lawyers, and progress is painfully slow. [16]

Some victims are clawing their way back via creative means. As previously mentioned, Daniel Leinhardt of Uganda runs a YouTube channel where he follows ongoing frauds, primarily crypto Ponzi schemes cut from the same cloth as OneCoin. Jen McAdam, the Glasgow woman who trusted OneCoin so much that she compelled her friends and family to invest over 250,000 euros, is writing a book about her quest to bring Dr. Ruja to justice. Countless others are working second, third, and even fourth jobs to refill their empty pockets, doing what's necessary to provide for their families and rebuild their shattered dreams.

Justice has come for many of OneCoin's leaders. Yet it has not rectified the stolen billions, and it may be a long time before any victims are made whole.

While most of OneCoin's elite have been forced to atone for their sins, one of them has not. One has somehow evaded capture and vanished completely.

And of all those who brought this misery upon the world, none is more sought after than Dr. Ruja Ignatova, the infamous fallen crypto queen.

7

Most Wanted

Dr. Ruja Ignatova's plan to "take the money and run and blame somebody else for this" went into motion in late October 2017.

On the 25th, Ignatova boarded a RyanAir plane in Sofia bound for Athens, Greece. The flight was uneventful and landed on time at its intended destination. Ignatova disembarked the plane, then promptly vanished from all public knowledge.

Where did she go?

Where is she, or where did she end up?

If she is alive, there is hope of bringing her to justice and making her victims whole again. Recent events have breathed life into that hope.

In the summer of 2022, the FBI added Dr. Ruja Ignatova to its Top Ten Most Wanted List, inflaming rumors that Ignatova was alive and living on a yacht somewhere. This theory intensified in January of 2023 when a listing appeared from a multi-million dollar London apartment, an economic act that forced her lawyers to list Ignatova as the active owner.

These clues are tantalizing and may ultimately lead to the crypto queen and her hiding place.

But others aren't so sure there's anyone to find. They've been following the money and the final breadcrumbs Ignatova left behind, and they lead to a very dark place.

So what's the answer?

Is Dr. Ruja alive or dead?

Last Words

When Dr. Ruja disappeared, she didn't completely vanish—at least not right away. There was one person with whom she exchanged messages after leaving the Athens airport: Her personal "fixer," Frank Schneider.

Schneider, a former spy for the tiny nation of Luxembourg, held an important role in Dr. Ruja's empire of deceit. He regularly solved problems by leveraging his espionage connections to keep Ignatova ahead of law enforcement and other threats to her business. He was also in charge of her personal security.

After landing in Athens, Ignatova texted Schneider that her bodyguard was returning to Bulgaria, and that she would be picked up soon by a group of unknown individuals. Since this wouldn't happen for several hours, she inferred that she'd kill the time shopping, one of her favorite pastimes.

What immediately surprised investigators about this exchange is the news that Ignatova's bodyguard returned to Sofia on someone else's orders—not hers, Schneider's, Greenwood's, or Konstantin's. That someone was likely connected to the arrangements for Ignatova's movements and placement once she vanished.

In the world of OneCoin, Dr. Ruja was the one giving the orders. There was no one to whom she showed fealty. Who, then, had the authority to order Ignatova's bodyguard away from her without her knowledge? In whom did she trust her safety, knowing she was about to disappear with over $4 billion in stolen riches?

No one knows who picked up the crypto queen and made her disappear. No official sightings, communications, or reports can confirm that Ignatova is still alive. Only one person, Frank Schneider, heard from her after her disappearance, and her final message is cryptic, and somewhat terrifying.

Hours after Ignatova's texts about shopping, Schneider received one final message:

"*Home safe.*"

If Schneider was worried about Ignatova's safety, this message didn't offer any reassurances. There was nothing wrong with the words; it was the language they were written in.

Throughout their professional relationship, Ignatova and Schneider regularly messaged one another in German, a language familiar to them both. Her communications about the bodyguard returning to Sofia, going shopping, and being picked up followed this pattern.

Yet the final message wasn't in German. It was in English.

After that, Schneider received nothing. [1]

Why would Ignatova send such a communication in English, betraying years of pattern and habit? One is hard-pressed to come up with a reason. With that in mind, it isn't hard to speculate that her phone was no longer in her possession, and this last text wasn't written by Ignatova at all. If that's the case, who wrote it and why?

This final exchange with Schneider makes perhaps the strongest argument that Dr. Ruja Ignatova isn't living it up on a yacht or partying day and night in the deserts of Dubai, but rather dead and disposed of, never to be found. Schneider himself seems to believe that this is how Ruja's story came to an end, stating, "I hope [she was not killed], but I haven't seen any evidence to the contrary." [2]

If that's the case, one wonders who would do such a thing to the crypto queen, and why. And if she *isn't* dead, as the FBI's recent update to the Most Wanted list suggests, who is hiding her?

How to Disappear

Shortly after Dr. Ruja vanished, the world began to see who Ignatova really was. It also had the chance to peek behind the carefully-guarded curtain of OneCoin's infrastructure and see what was going on.

To consider where and how Dr. Ruja disappeared, one must first understand the web of shell companies and financial pipelines that formed the foundation of the OneCoin empire. It was enormous, with dummy corporations and asset management companies set up all over Europe, Asia, Africa, and the Caribbean to manage the numerous properties OneCoin used to launder its illegal earnings. The structure mirrors that of organized crime, making investigation and prosecution all the more difficult. This similarity might not be by accident.

Perhaps Ignatova's most infamous connection to the world of organized crime is Hristofos Amanatidis, or "Taki," a fellow Bulgarian nicknamed "The Cocaine King." The connections between Amanatidis and OneCoin are deliberately difficult to trace, but financial investigators have been able to piece together a map that shows the intricate relationship between the two criminal organizations. Amanatidis's support of the OneCoin empire was undoubtedly helpful in providing cash to pay out the top-tier MLM promoters, a necessary evil of maintaining a Ponzi scheme.[3]

As of this writing in 2023, Taki's location is unknown, having left Bulgaria to elude authorities. It's possible that Ignatova is working with the kingpin to stay underground, moving around just like an on-the-run gangster to evade capture.

It's also possible Taki decided to tie up a loose end and stab her in the back.

Two weeks prior to vanishing, Dr. Ruja received a damning piece of intelligence: The FBI was investigating OneCoin. She learned this in rather dramatic fashion, too.

Ignatova called Gilbert Armenta, her South Florida money launderer and lover. Eager to hear that he would be moving on from his marriage, Ignatova pressed him to split from his wife so they could run away together. But the conversation did not go as planned.

"I don't deserve this, and [your wife] does not deserve this," Ignatova protested in an audio recording made available by the U.S. Attorney's Office. "And ... [if] you think you are smarter than anyone, it's not [cool]. You understand? It's just not. It's not cool. There's one thing that's called personal integrity. Google it." [4]

Not only would Armenta not leave his wife, but he responded to Ruja with terse, nervous phrases. He was clearly on edge and chose his words carefully. Ignatova sniffed out the truth: Armenta was cooperating with the FBI.

This sordid dialogue wasn't Ignatova's only tip. Allegations suggest that highly-placed Bulgarian officials were on OneCoin's payroll. Hours after an international meeting with Europol and the FBI about the cryptocurrency's alleged crimes, Ignatova received word that she was in the crosshairs of an FBI investigation that was progressing with great speed. [5]

For Ignatova's criminal partners, this must have presented a quandary. Should they protect their golden goose and keep her safe after so many years of financial windfall? Or had she become a liability that might lead to more arrests and even take down their vast criminal cartel?

For a character like Taki, a figure in the mold of villains from *Breaking Bad* or *The Wire*, one question must have been dominant: Could Ignatova stand up to FBI pressure? Or would she spill the secrets of his Bulgarian drug ring to avoid a lifetime in American federal prison?

Circumstantial evidence suggests that Taki took the matter into his own hands, evidence that comes directly from the testimony of her brother, Konstantin.

When Konstantin was finally arrested in Los Angeles in 2019, he quickly capitulated to the FBI's demands that he work with them to find his sister. However, this act wasn't without terrible risk. According to Dr. Jonathan Levy's petition, "Konstantin Ignatov... indicated that he believed his life was in danger from organized crime. Ignatov testified that he had been abducted on at least two occasions and threatened twice at gunpoint by criminal gangs involved with OneCoin including the Hell's Angels in Zurich and Bulgarian organized crime in Sofia. As part of his plea agreement with the United States, Ignatov seeks to enter the witness protection program along with his girlfriend and child." Recent reporting from Bulgarian news outlets claim that Taki had Ruja murdered on his yacht in 2018, based on documents found on the body of a murdered police officer. [6, 7, 8]

These developments don't bode well for the crypto queen's prospects.

There is still a chance that she is in the midst of an Eastern European mob, protected by the umbrella of discretion that often accompanies organized crime. If this is true, she is almost certainly complicit in the threats against her brother. A living Dr. Ruja, on the run for over five years, will have abandoned every familial connection and relationship in order to survive, including ties to her infant daughter. As Ruja has hidden in the shadows, every OneCoin associate and accomplice has surrendered or been arrested; no one, not even her one-time boyfriend Greenwood or flesh-and-blood brother Konstantin, has been worth saving.

All of this assumes she is alive *and* acting on her own accord. As of this writing, the truth is unknown; her being alive and dead are both possible. In a way, Dr. Ruja Ignatova is like Schroedinger's famous cat: She is both alive and dead at the same time. [9]

Easy Money

There are other theories and possibilities regarding Ignatova's location that don't require her to be dead or hiding with the Bulgarian mafia. One such theory places her in Russia. [10]

The Russians are well known for harboring dangerous characters and sponsoring international campaigns of fraud and deception. Their ability to influence and meddle in foreign elections has been well documented. Based on transcripts of Ignatova's conversations with Armenta, she had connections to Russia's cybercrime resources and used them to get her hands on privileged information.

Speaking to Armenta about how easily the FBI could access his emails, she said, "Gilbert, we can get access to your emails between now and 24 hours if we want to. You cannot prevent this shit. You have to be fucking careful. What these Russian guys can do, you cannot imagine. I mean, if they can do it, everybody can do it."

Ignatova went on to urge Armenta to only communicate with her face-to-face or through encrypted phone conversations. "Nothing else is safe," she urged. "Just believe me. I can get everything I want within 24 hours. And if I can, they can too." [11]

Ironically, this conversation itself was recorded and analyzed by the FBI, with whom Armenta had been cooperating for weeks. But it didn't tell the Americans anything they didn't already know, and Ignatova would soon vanish and never speak to Armenta again.

The Russia theory makes for an intriguing possibility. Given the enmeshment between Russian oligarchs and fraudulent revenue streams, it is certainly feasible that Dr. Ruja is strutting the streets of Moscow in an ushanka.

However, the FBI adding Ignatova to their Most Wanted list in summer 2022 makes it less likely than ever that Ignatova is hiding in Putin's shadow. At the time the FBI made its public announcement, Russia was several months into an unprovoked war with Ukraine, rattling its nuclear saber and raking the nerves of every nation in NATO. If the FBI was hoping for a rogue Russian citizen to blow the whistle on an incognito Ignatova, July of 2022 seemed like a poor time to do it, given the way Russian authorities treat political dissidents.

For this reason, it's difficult to suspect that Ignatova is stashed in a Siberian bunker. It's easier, however, to imagine her living large in an Emirati mansion.

The United Arab Emirates has worked tirelessly to polish its international image in the last few decades. Constructing a modern metropolis in Dubai featuring the world's tallest building, the UAE has seen its tourism industry explode. Like other nations on the Arabian peninsula, the UAE is a hybrid theocracy and oligarchy of oil barons and extremely wealthy sheiks, heads of royal families that date back centuries. One such sheik is His Excellency Faisal Bin Sultan Bin Salem Al Qassimi, whose son Saoud made Dr. Ruja Ignatova a billionaire. [12]

Thanks to her connections to other highly-positioned people, Ignatova and Saoud formed a beneficial partnership early in OneCoin's history. Through Ignatova, Saoud gained access to OneCoin's profits when she opened accounts in the UAE to hold the company's laundered gains. In return, Ignatova received the UAE's blessing to travel and reside there as she pleased, providing a haven from the scrutinizing eye of the Western World.

In 2015, Dr. Ruja made Saoud an offer he couldn't refuse. In exchange for unlimited access to all of OneCoin's bank accounts in the United Arab Emirates, as well as some real estate in the country, Dr. Ruja asked for payment in Bitcoin. He complied by giving her four USB drives holding 230,000 units of the digital currency, valued at roughly $50 million USD in 2015. At the time, it was a relatively fair exchange for the amount of money stored in OneCoin's UAE coffers. However, those Bitcoins skyrocketed in value not long after Ignatova disappeared. Today they are worth more than $5 billion USD, and before the COVID-19 pandemic of ensuing economic downturn, the total was much higher. [13]

This creates a solid link between Dr. Ruja and the UAE. While the OneCoin accounts were frozen in 2015 due to suspicions surrounding the company, they were later unfrozen and used to purchase a $20 million condominium, according to documents leaked to Jamie Bartlett for *The Missing CryptoQueen* podcast. As it was with the recent apartment listing in London, Dr. Ruja's name was on the property deed. However, being on a deed has not produced a living, breathing Dr. Ruja, so the evidence is spurious at best. [14]

Another clue tantalized investigators when, prior to his arrest, Konstantin took a selfie from somewhere in Dubai and posted it to social media. Intrigued that this might be

MOST WANTED   107

a hint as to Ruja's location, Bartlett and his team chased the lead as far as possible, even recruiting software analysts to identify the precise location where the photograph was taken. Their efforts hit a wall when it came time to investigate the house they located. Despite putting up a shiny facade of a modern, capitalist society, the United Arab Emirates is not friendly to journalists, especially those from outside the country, making the matter difficult to resolve. Even if Bartlett and his team were to close in on the property and knock on the door, Ignatova would likely know of their presence days in advance, thanks to her connections in the government.[15]

Given Ignatova's deep financial connections to the UAE, there's a strong chance that she is there or has spent a significant amount of time hiding under the protection of the sheiks. There is also a chance that the BitCoin deal soured the UAE rulers' opinion of Dr. Ruja Ignatova, and they decided to wash their hands of her.

No one knows what happened to the four USB drives holding the 230,000 Bitcoin. Thanks to the anonymity of cryptocurrency, no one knows if or how Ignatova spent her riches. It's not beyond imagination to think that Saoud, his father, or the other influential leaders of the UAE came to believe that they had been conned by Ignatova's schemes and decided to deal with the matter once and for all.

Wherever she went after October 25th, 2017, and wherever she might be, Dr. Ruja Ignatova has still not been found. All we have left are pieces with which to speculate.

But we do know that there are millions of dollars of goods—cash, real estate, and other assets—that are still tied to Dr. Ruja in the United Arab Emirates, and a lot of people want to get their hands on them.

The Fall of the Queen

Ruja Ignatova always wanted to be rich.

According to those who knew her as a young woman, Ruja obsessed over the niceties of life. She devoted hours to her personal appearances each day, preparing a carefully curated image for the world to see. That image projected success, competence, and glamor. [16]

Between 2014 and 2017, it worked like a charm.

Now, Dr. Ruja can no longer run her scams in the open. She no longer dazzles her marks with glittering gowns, bright lipstick, and twinkling jewelry. Her confident voice no longer preaches salvation by OneCoin.

The crypto queen has truly fallen.

If she is alive, however, she is working a new con: Concealing her identity.

Without a doubt, a surviving Ignatova has had to adapt to the global manhunt closing around her. According to a *Newsweek* report, a German police force has been searching for Ignatova since 2020 and now believes she has had facial reconstructive surgery to alter her appearance. The report suggests that Ignatova may have even changed her gender and used hormones to grow facial hair. [17]

While tantalizing, a hair-raising claim such as this forgets something fundamental about Ruja Ignatova: Her nature.

Every element of her rise; every scam she pulled from a factory town in Westphalia to the stadiums of London; every moment she was on camera: It put her at the center of attention. Dr. Ruja, the crypto queen, *was* the product.

Everything else was there to justify throwing money at her so she could have what she wanted, whenever she wanted it.

"There were many cultish things that the company did," crypto enthusiast Timothy Curry explained on *The Missing CryptoQueen*. "Everything to [sic] the musical introductions, to Ruja, to the theatrics, they really did create a worship behind her. People would be like 'Bless you Ruja, God bless you.' It became worship." [18]

We've heard this testimony before, and it's worth revisiting as we close the curtain on Ruja's story. The crypto queen didn't resign herself to a crooked life of scamming people from the confines of a smoky office. That was Ponzi and Madoff's preferred approach. For Ignatova, it seems that such an existence wouldn't be enough. She needed celebrity and spotlight as much as she needed oxygen. Every day of her life, Ruja Ignatova directed her energy toward elevating her status. Like the ancient kings of Persia, Babylon, and Rome, all of whom were convinced of their own deity status, Ignatova set her gaze beyond the paltry veil of boring, ordinary life. Regular day-to-day existence wasn't nearly enough to sustain her.

Instead, she adopted an attitude that acted as if ordinary people were there to serve her and raise her up to her destined perch. How else can one explain the wanton cruelty and deceit? How else can we reckon with her utter disdain for her "investors," her deliberate design of OneCoin to defraud as many people worldwide as possible, her specific targeting of minority and impoverished communities, and her willingness—if still alive—to let her friends, partners, and lovers take the fall while she continued to enjoy the spoils in secret?[19]

If Dr. Ruja is still alive, she is almost certainly still chasing her own greatness. It's extremely unlikely she submitted herself to gender reassignment simply because such an act betrays every other choice she has made. A person such as Dr. Ruja Ignatova can only continue to bask in the comforts of luxury, even if they are borrowed and financed with blood money. Those around her are likely well-paid for their silence, welcomed into the embrace of the OneCoin matriarch and allowed to partake in similar pleasures, all under the threat of unspeakable punishment for violating trust. They are certainly the kind of people who know how to keep secrets: Agents of hostile governments or criminal henchmen who would rather die than turn rat.

Such a network is difficult and expensive to maintain. But with the billions reaped from her deal with Saoud bin Faisal Al Qassimi, Ignatova could hold out for several lifetimes, especially if she's found ways to invest those profits and live off the interest.

When the crypto queen abdicated her throne in 2017, it didn't take long for the OneCoin empire to come crashing down. Its leaders scrambled to keep the scam running, sucking every dollar possible from remaining prospects. When the law came for them, they scattered like roaches and tried to hide, failing one-by-one until only one remained at large. That one remains, as-yet unaccounted for.

Is she still alive?

Rumors abound and alleged sightings are reported everyday. But after half a decade, no one can confirm that

Dr. Ruja still walks among the living. Just the same, no one can prove otherwise.

Dr. Ruja Ignatova is a ghost, and whether that ghost will ever appear again is—for now—a mystery.

Afterword

The true number of victims defrauded by OneCoin may never be known. All around the world, everyday citizens are picking up the pieces that Greenwood and the Ignatovas left behind, trying to find justice in some way, shape, or form.

If you, a loved one, or someone in your community invested in OneCoin and have yet to find restitution, there are resources available. While none can fully guarantee that you will be made completely whole, many of these individuals, groups, and organizations are working tirelessly to bring the perpetrators of OneCoin to justice and see that justice is done for people like you.

Here are a few resources that may help you on your journey:

- **The Facebook Group for OneCoin survivors**, led by Jennifer McAdam, can be found at the link below. Please be prepared to share your story or the story of the loved one you're connected to in order to gain access to this group of people: https://www.facebook.com/groups/1270760729671878/

- **The Law Firm of Schlun and Elseven** in Germany has a website with information for those who are seeking legal remedies to crimes against them by OneCoin: https://se-legal.de/onecoin-scam-german-lawyers-representing-fraud-victims/?lang=en

- Download and view the **FBI Wanted Poster for Dr. Ruja Ignatova** here: https://www.fbi.gov/wanted/topten/ruja-ignatova/@@download.pdf

- **The Department of Justice (USA)** has shared multiple postings about the progress of the OneCoin prosecutions. Find more information here: https://www.justice.gov/usao-sdny/pr/bulgarian-woman-charged-role-multi-billion-dollar-cryptocurrency-pyramid-scheme-onecoin

Notes

Sources and Citations

Introduction

1. Cryptoslav, Ivan. "The OneCoin Scam: the Dazzling Story of the Biggest Crypto Ponzi in History." *Alexandria*, published by *CoinMarketCap.com*, August, 2022. https://coinmarketcap.com/alexandria/article/the-onecoin-scam-the-dazzling-story-of-the-biggest-crypto-ponzi-in-history

2. Many journalistic outlets have reported with no uncertainty that OneCoin was and is nothing more than a scam. One such report comes from AP News:

   "Bogus 'Bitcoin killer' cryptocurrency founder pleads guilty." 16 December, 2022, AP *News*. https://apnews.com/article/business-manhattan-fraud-429904f53ead84144532eb3a282a7845

3. Ibid.

4. Levy, Dr. Jonathan. "Before the Republic of Bulgaria Office of the Constitutional Ombudsman: Petition of Dr. Jonathan Levy in the matter of OneCoin," 16 November 2021. https://www.jlevy.co/wp-content/uploads/2021/11/Petititon-16162021-J-Levy.pdf

5. Aronczyk, Amanda. "'CryptoQueen' Ruja Ignatova's international scheme landed her on FBI's Most Wanted," *All Things Considered* radio program. NPR, 8 July, 2022. https://www.npr.org/2022/07/08/1110577425/cryptoqueen-ruja-ignatovas-international-scheme-landed-her-on-fbis-most-wanted

6. Hamilton, Brad. "Inside the life and crimes of the new addition to the FBI's 10 Most Wanted Ruja Ignatova." *New York Post*, 10 August, 2022. https://nypost.com/2022/08/10/the-life-and-crimes-of-ruja-ignatova-new-to-fbis-10-most-wanted-ruja-ignatova/

Chapter 1: "We Create the World"

1. Duggan, Wayne. "The History of Bitcoin, the First Cryptocurrency." *U.S. News and World Report*, 31 August 2022. https://money.usnews.com/investing/articles/the-history-of-bitcoin

2. Greenberg, Andy. "Most Criminal Cryptocurrency Funnels Through Just 5 Exchanges." *Wired.com*, 26 January

NOTES   117

2023. https://www.wired.com/story/cryptocurrency-money-laundering-chainalysis-report/

3. Many markets have their own FOMO phenomenon, and there are many resources available to learn more about it (and how to avoid falling prey to it). One such article is this excellent piece:

    Opeyemi Amure, Tobi. "How to Deal With Crypto FOMO." Fact checked by Velasquez, Vikki. *Investopidea.com*, 14 September 2022. https://www.investopedia.com/deal-with-crypto-fomo-6455103

4. Amadeo, Kimberly. "2008 Financial Crisis: Causes, Costs, and Whether It Could Happen Again." *TheBalanceMoney.com*, 10 February 2022. https://www.thebalancemoney.com/2008-financial-crisis-3305679

5. Hamilton, Brad. "Inside the life and crimes of the new addition to the FBI's 10 Most Wanted Ruja Ignatova." *New York Post*, 10 August, 2022. https://nypost.com/2022/08/10/the-life-and-crimes-of-ruja-ignatova-new-to-fbis-10-most-wanted-ruja-ignatova/

6. OneCoin and Ignatova, Dr. Ruja. "The Blockchain." *YouTube*, 11 June 2016. https://www.youtube.com/watch?v=638_Jpp2Rq8&t=1874s&ab_channel=OneCoin

7. Bartlett, Jamie, presenter and narrator. "Dr. Ruja," *The Missing CryptoQueen*, season 1,

episode 1. *The BBC*, 19 September 2019. https://podcasts.apple.com/us/podcast/episode-1-dr-ruja/id1480370173?i=1000450368895

8. Hamilton, Brad. "Inside the life and crimes of the new addition to the FBI's 10 Most Wanted Ruja Ignatova." *New York Post*, 10 August, 2022. https://nypost.com/2022/08/10/the-life-and-crimes-of-ruja-ignatova-new-to-fbis-10-most-wanted-ruja-ignatova/

9. Ibid.

Chapter 2: "The Cult and Its Queen"

1. Farley, Robert and St. Petersburg Times. "Scientologists' policy toward outcasts under fire." *The Orlando Sentinel*, 26 June 2006. https://www.orlandosentinel.com/news/os-xpm-2006-06-26-scientology26-story.html

2. Bartlett, Jamie, presenter and narrator. "Dr. Ruja," *The Missing CryptoQueen*, season 1, episode 1. *The BBC*, 17 October 2019. https://podcasts.apple.com/us/podcast/episode-1-dr-ruja/id1480370173?i=1000450368895

3. Bartlett, Jamie, presenter and narrator. "The Bitcoin Killer," *The Missing CryptoQueen*, season 1, episode 2. *The BBC*, 19 September 2019. https://podcasts.apple.com/us/podcast/episode-2-the-bitcoin-killer/id1480370173?i=1000450368896

4. Ibid.

5. Angel, Devanie. "The Power of Cults: How Chico State Prof. Janja Lalich went from cult member to author-expert." *Chico News & Review*, 12 August 2004. https://www.newsreview.com/chico/content/the-power-of-cults/31494/

6. Lalich, Janja and Tobias, Madeleine. *Take Back Your Life: Recovering from Cults and Abusive Relationships*. Bay Tree Publishing, 17 August 2006. Retrieved from https://janjalalich.com/help/characteristics-associated-with-cults/

7. Bartlett, Jamie, presenter and narrator. "More than just a coin," *The Missing CryptoQueen*, season 1, episode 3. The BBC, 26 September 2019. https://podcasts.apple.com/us/podcast/episode-3-more-than-just-a-coin/id1480370173?i=1000451348496

8. Ibid.

9. "Democratic Workers Party." *Wikipedia*. Retrieved 16 January 2023. https://en.wikipedia.org/wiki/Democratic_Workers_Party

10. OneCoin and Ignatova, Dr. Ruja. "The Blockchain." *YouTube*, 11 June 2016. https://www.youtube.com/watch?v=638_Jpp2Rq8&t=1874s&ab_channel=OneCoin

11. Bartlett, Jamie, presenter and narrator. "More than just a coin," *The Missing CryptoQueen*, season 1,

episode 3. *The BBC*, 26 September 2019. https://podcasts.apple.com/us/podcast/episode-3-more-than-just-a-coin/id1480370173?i=1000451348496

12. "Subpoenaed emails reveal OneCoin was fraudulent from inception." *BehindMLM.com*, 9 March 2019. https://behindmlm.com/companies/onecoin/subpoenaed-emails-reveal-onecoin-was-fraudulent-from-inception/

13. Ibid.

14. Manoukian, Marina. "The Untold Story of the CryptoQueen." *Grunge.com*, 9 September 2022. https://www.grunge.com/918216/the-untold-story-of-the-cryptoqueen/

15. Ösp, Auðr. "Ásdís Robbery and the embezzlement case – Waiting for a call from the alleged embezzler: 'I don't want to believe she's dead.'" *DV (Dagblaðið Vísir)*, 28 November 2019. https://www.dv.is/frettir/2019/11/28/asdis-ran-flaekt-eitt-staersta-fjarsvikamal-sidari-ara/

16. Hamilton, Brad. "Inside the life and crimes of the new addition to the FBI's 10 Most Wanted Ruja Ignatova." *New York Post*, 10 August, 2022. https://nypost.com/2022/08/10/the-life-and-crimes-of-ruja-ignatova-new-to-fbis-10-most-wanted-ruja-ignatova/

Chapter 3: The Gospel of Gold

1. Spin Mukasa, Robert. "Con bishop steals billions from Ugandans." *The Observer*, 26 August 2020. https://observer.ug/news/headlines/66287-con-bishop-steals-billions-from-ugandans

2. "Uganda National Household Survey (2019/20 UNHS)." Uganda Bureau of Statistics, August 2021. https://www.ubos.org/wp-content/uploads/publications/09_2021Uganda-National-Survey-Report-2019-2020.pdf

3. Interview with Daniel Leinhardt, 19 January 2023.

4. "Ugandan OneCoin kingpin John Mwambusya arrested." *BehindMLM.com*, 1 February 2022. https://behindmlm.com/companies/onecoin/ugandan-onecoin-kingpin-john-mwambusya-arrested/

5. Leinhardt, Daniel. *YouTube*, 9 March 2023. https://www.youtube.com/@DanielLeinhardt

6. "Clarification – OneCoin Certification." Centre of Islamic Banking & Economics, 28 November 2016. http://alhudacibe.com/pressrelease75.php

7. Bartlett, Jamie. "How the world's biggest crypto-scam targeted British Muslims." *The Spectator*, 21 October 2019. https://www.spectator.co.uk/article/how-the-world-s-biggest-crypto-scam-targeted-british-musli

ms/

8. In its rebuttals to claims made by Barlett, Jamie on *The Missing CryptoQueen* podcast, OneCoin stated: "OneCoin verifiably fulfills all criteria of the definition of a cryptocurrency. Its value is confirmed and reflects a constant worldwide trading activities such as a DealShaker platform, one of the major global trading platforms and elsewhere."

9. Bartlett, Jamie, presenter and narrator. "More than just a coin," *The Missing CryptoQueen*, season 1, episode 3. The BBC, 26 September 2019. https://podcasts.apple.com/us/podcast/episode-3-more-than-just-a-coin/id1480370173?i=100045 1348496

10. Lee, Sam. "OneCoin: Remembering the Scam That Hit China Hardest." *AsiaCryptoToday.com*, 19 March 2019. https://www.asiacryptotoday.com/onecoin-remembering-the-scam-that-hit-china-hardest/

Chapter 4: Weaponizing Hope

1. Trex, Ethan. "Who was Ponzi – what the heck was his scheme?" CNN.*com*, 23 December 2008. http://edition.cnn.com/2008/LIVING/wayoflife/12/23/mf.ponzi.scheme/

2. Additional information in this section taken from: "Charles Ponzi." *Wikipedia*. Retrieved 25 February 2023. https://en.wikipedia.org/wiki/Charles_Ponzi

3. Hamilton, Brad. "Inside the life and crimes of the new addition to the FBI's 10 Most Wanted Ruja Ignatova." *New York Post*, 10 August, 2022. https://nypost.com/2022/08/10/the-life-and-crimes-of-ruja-ignatova-new-to-fbis-10-most-wanted-ruja-ignatova/

4. U.S. Attorney's Office, Southern District of New York. "Co-Founder Of Multi-Billion-Dollar Cryptocurrency Pyramid Scheme "OneCoin" Pleads Guilty." United States Department of Justice, 16 December 2022. https://www.justice.gov/usao-sdny/pr/co-founder-multi-billion-dollar-cryptocurrency-pyramid-scheme-onecoin-pleads-guilty

5. Ibid.

6. Hayes, Adam. "Bernie Madoff: Who He Was, How His Ponzi Scheme Worked." Reviewed by Khartit, Khadija and face checked by Ecker, Jared. *Investopedia.com*, 8 September 2022. https://www.investopedia.com/terms/b/bernard-madoff.asp

7. Kay, Grace and Yang, Stephanie. "Bernie Madoff died in prison after carrying out the largest Ponzi scheme in history – here's how it worked." *Insider.com*, 14 April 2021. https://www.businessinsider.com/how-bernie-madoffs-ponzi-scheme-worked-2014-7

8. Manoukian, Marina. "The Untold Story of the CryptoQueen." *Grunge.com*, 9 September

2022. https://www.grunge.com/918216/the-untold-story-of-the-cryptoqueen/

9. Multiple sources have reported on the language Ignatova and Greenwood used when referring to their users/victims, including the DOJ report:

U.S. Attorney's Office, Southern District of New York. "Co-Founder Of Multi-Billion-Dollar Cryptocurrency Pyramid Scheme "OneCoin" Pleads Guilty." United States Department of Justice, 16 December 2022. https://www.justice.gov/usao-sdny/pr/co-founder-multi-billion-dollar-cryptocurrency-pyramid-scheme-onecoin-pleads-guilty

Chapter 5: "There is No Blockchain."

1. Bartlett, Jamie, presenter and narrator. "The Bitcoin Killer," *The Missing CryptoQueen*, season 1, episode 2. The BBC, 19 September 2019. https://podcasts.apple.com/us/podcast/episode-2-the-bitcoin-killer/id1480370173?i=1000450368896

2. OneCoin and Ignatova, Dr. Ruja. "The Blockchain." *YouTube*, 11 June 2016. https://www.youtube.com/watch?v=638_Jpp2Rq8&t=1874s&ab_channel=OneCoin

3. Ibid.

4. Ibid.

5. A wealth of resources are available to learn more about blockchain and how it prevents double-spending, including:
Bansal, Druti. "Double Spending and How It's Prevented by Blockchain." *Topcoder.com*, 7 October 2022. https://www.topcoder.com/thrive/articles/double-spending-and-how-its-prevented-by-blockchain

6. "Dacxi Review: Ed Ludbrook's DAC Ponzi points." *BehindMLM.com*, 13 October 2019. https://behindmlm.com/mlm-reviews/dacxi-review-ed-ludbrooks-dac-ponzi-points/

7. Bjerke has expressed tangible dread over his decision to blow the whistle on OneCoin, and carefully dodged certain questions about the people behind OneCoin and Dr. Ruja's success during his interviews with Jamie Bartlett:

Bartlett, Jamie, presenter and narrator. "The Bitcoin Killer," *The Missing CryptoQueen*, season 1, episode 2. The BBC, 19 September 2019. https://podcasts.apple.com/us/podcast/episode-2-the-bitcoin-killer/id1480370173?i=1000450368896

8. Bartlett, Jamie, presenter and narrator. "Dr. Ruja," *The Missing CryptoQueen*, season 1, episode 1. The BBC, 19 September 2019. https://podcasts.apple.com/us/podcast/ep

isode-1-dr-ruja/id1480370173?i=1000450368895

9. OneCoin and Ignatova, Dr. Ruja. "Dr. Ruja Ignatova at the Fourth EU-Southeast Europe Summit. Countdown to Stability and Growth?" *YouTube*, 22 October 2015. https://www.youtube.com/watch?v=TpcIDMXA5_0&ab_channel=OneCoin

10. OneCoin and Ignatova, Dr. Ruja. "The Blockchain." *YouTube*, 11 June 2016. https://www.youtube.com/watch?v=638_Jpp2Rq8&t=1874s&ab_channel=OneCoin

Chapter 6: Justice for Some

1. U.S. Attorney's Office, Southern District of New York. "Co-Founder Of Multi-Billion-Dollar Cryptocurrency Pyramid Scheme "OneCoin" Pleads Guilty." United States Department of Justice, 16 December 2022. https://www.justice.gov/usao-sdny/pr/co-founder-multi-billion-dollar-cryptocurrency-pyramid-scheme-onecoin-pleads-guilty

2. "Subpoenaed emails reveal OneCoin was fraudulent from inception." *BehindMLM.com*, 9 March 2019. https://behindmlm.com/companies/onecoin/subpoenaed-emails-reveal-onecoin-was-fraudulent-from-inception/

3. U.S. Attorney's Office, Southern District of New York. "Co-Founder Of Multi-Billion-Dollar

Cryptocurrency Pyramid Scheme "OneCoin" Pleads Guilty." United States Department of Justice, 16 December 2022. https://www.justice.gov/usao-sdny/pr/co-founder-multi-billion-dollar-cryptocurrency-pyramid-scheme-onecoin-pleads-guilty

4. Hamilton, Brad. "Inside the life and crimes of the new addition to the FBI's 10 Most Wanted Ruja Ignatova." *New York Post*, 10 August, 2022. https://nypost.com/2022/08/10/the-life-and-crimes-of-ruja-ignatova-new-to-fbis-10-most-wanted-ruja-ignatova/

5. Tassev, Lubomir. "Onecoin Victims Petition Bulgaria for Seizure of Assets and Compensation." *Bitcoin.com*, 19 November 2021. https://news.bitcoin.com/onecoin-victims-petition-bulgaria-for-seizure-of-assets-and-compensation/

6. Bartlett, Jamie, presenter and narrator. "Dr. Ruja," *The Missing CryptoQueen*, season 1, episode 1. The BBC, 19 September 2019. https://podcasts.apple.com/us/podcast/episode-1-dr-ruja/id1480370173?i=1000450368895

7. Ibid.

8. Manoukian, Marina. "The Untold Story of the CryptoQueen." *Grunge.com*, 9 September 2022. https://www.grunge.com/918216/the-untold-story-of-the-cryptoqueen/

9. U.S. Attorney's Office, Southern District of New York. "Co-Founder Of Multi-Billion-Dollar Cryptocurrency Pyramid Scheme "OneCoin" Pleads Guilty." United States Department of Justice, 16 December 2022. https://www.justice.gov/usao-sdny/pr/co-founder-multi-billion-dollar-cryptocurrency-pyramid-scheme-onecoin-pleads-guilty

10. Ibid.

11. Frankel, Alison. "In $4 billion OneCoin fraud, jurisdiction dooms claims against ex-Big Law partner." *Reuters*, 22 September 2021. https://www.reuters.com/legal/litigation/4-billion-onecoin-fraud-jurisdiction-dooms-claims-against-ex-big-law-partner-2021-09-22/

12. Helms, Kevin. "8 People Arrested in Argentina Linked to Onecoin Ponzi Scam." *Bitcoin.com*, 13 December 2020. https://news.bitcoin.com/8-people-arrested-argentina-onecoin-ponzi-scam/

13. Sinclair, Sebastian. "Promoters of Crypto Ponzi Scheme OneCoin Murdered in Mexico." *CoinDesk.com*, 15 July 2020. https://www.coindesk.com/markets/2020/07/15/promoters-of-crypto-ponzi-scheme-onecoin-murdered-in-mexico/

14. Igor Alberts claims to have not known that OneCoin was a scam while he and his wife, Andreea Cimbala, made millions off of it. Some journalists and watch

dogs are skeptical, as in this article:

"To promote DagCoin, Igor Alberts slams Ponzi he earned millions in." *BehindMLM.com*, 13 January 2018. https://behindmlm.com/companies/to-promote-dagcoin-igor-alberts-slams-ponzi-he-earned-millions-in/

15. Levy, Dr. Jonathan. "Before the Republic of Bulgaria Office of the Constitutional Ombudsman: Petition of Dr. Jonathan Levy in the matter of OneCoin," 16 November 2021. https://www.jlevy.co/wp-content/uploads/2021/11/Petititon-16162021-J-Levy.pdf

16. "Ruja Ignatova's attorneys claim UK penthouse on her behalf." *BehindMLM.com*, 14 January 2023. https://behindmlm.com/companies/onecoin/ruja-ignatovas-attorneys-claim-uk-penthouse-on-her-behalf/

Chapter 7: Most Wanted

1. "Bulgarian Authorities were Telling Cryptoqueen Ruja Ignatova When it was Safe to Return." *Novinite.com Sofia New Agency*, 19 August 2022. https://www.novinite.com/articles/216358/Bulgarian+Authorities+were+Telling+Cryptoqueen+Ruja+Ignatova+When+it+was+Safe+to+Return

2. Ibid.

3. Bartlett, Jamie. "Why I believe the Cryptoqueen

fraudster who vanished with £3.3BN is hiding on a yacht in the Med: Investigator who spent years hunting Bulgarian Ruja Ignatova reveals his theory as she becomes only woman on FBI's most wanted list." *The Daily Mail*, 3 July 2022. https://www.dailymail.co.uk/news/article-10976211/Why-believe-Cryptoqueen-fraudster-vanished-3-3billion-hiding-luxury-yacht-Med.html

4. Russell Lee, Matthew. "OneCoin Ruja Ignatova Wiretapped Gilbert Armenta And Found Spineless Cooperator Before Disappearing." *InnerCityPress.com*, 12 November 2019. https://www.innercitypress.com/sdny24onecoinignatovcrim111219.html

5. Levy, Dr. Jonathan. "Before the Republic of Bulgaria Office of the Constitutional Ombudsman: Petition of Dr. Jonathan Levy in the matter of OneCoin," 16 November 2021. https://www.jlevy.co/wp-content/uploads/2021/11/Petititon-16162021-J-Levy.pdf

6. Ibid.

7. Nelson, Jason. "Bulgarian Investigators Claim 'Cryptoqueen' Was Murdered in 2018." *Decrypt.co*, 21 February 2023. https://decrypt.co/121879/bulgarian-investigators-claim-cryptoqueen-ruja-ignatova-was-killed-in-2018

8. Numerous investigations have identified connections between OneCoin and Eastern European organized crime, including:

"Hearing transcript confirms OneCoin's ties to European organized crime." *BehindMLM.com*, 28 June 2019. https://behindmlm.com/companies/onecoin/hearing-transcript-confirms-onecoins-ties-to-european-organized-crime/

9. "Ruja Ignatova being murdered in 2018 is unlikely." *BehindMLM.com*, 23 February 2023. https://behindmlm.com/companies/onecoin/ruja-ignatova-being-murdered-in-2018-is-unlikely/

10. Russell Lee, Matthew. "OneCoin Ruja Ignatova Wiretapped Gilbert Armenta And Found Spineless Cooperator Before Disappearing." *InnerCityPress.com*, 12 November 2019. https://www.innercitypress.com/sdny24onecoinignatovcrim111219.html

11. Russell Lee, Matthew. "OneCoin Ruja Ignatova Told Gilbert Armenta To Watch Out For Russian Guys Before Disappearing." *InnerCityPress.com*, 12 November 2019. https://www.innercitypress.com/sdny24onecoinignatovcrim111219.html

12. Steves, Rick. "Lawsuit Reveals OneCoin Scammer 'CryptoQueen' Holds 230,000 BTC Worth $13 Billion." *FinanceFeeds.com*, 13 May 2021. https://financefeeds.com/lawsuit-reveals-onecoin-scammer-cryptoqueen-holds-230000-btc-worth-13-billion/

13. Ibid.

14. Bartlett, Jamie, presenter and narrator. "The Dubai Files," *The Missing CryptoQueen*, season 1, episode 10. The BBC, 28 September 2022. https://podcasts.apple.com/us/podcast/episode-10-the-dubai-files/id1480370173?i=1000580876187

15. Ibid.

16. Hamilton, Brad. "Inside the life and crimes of the new addition to the FBI's 10 Most Wanted Ruja Ignatova." *New York Post*, 10 August, 2022. https://nypost.com/2022/08/10/the-life-and-crimes-of-ruja-ignatova-new-to-fbis-10-most-wanted-ruja-ignatova/

17. McGee, William for Zenger News. "New Look: Missing Crypto Queen May Have Surgically Changed Appearance to Avoid Capture." *Newsweek.com*, 13 May 2022. https://www.newsweek.com/new-look-missing-crypto-queen-may-have-surgically-changed-appearance-avoid-capture-1706520

18. Bartlett, Jamie, presenter and narrator. "More than just a coin," *The Missing CryptoQueen*, season 1, episode 3. The BBC, 26 September 2019. https://podcasts.apple.com/us/podcast/episode-3-more-than-just-a-coin/id1480370173?i=1000451348496

19. U.S. Attorney's Office, Southern District of New York. "Co-Founder Of Multi-Billion-Dollar

Cryptocurrency Pyramid Scheme "OneCoin" Pleads Guilty." United States Department of Justice, 16 December 2022. https://www.justice.gov/usao-sdny/pr/co-founder-multi-billion-dollar-cryptocurrency-pyramid-scheme-onecoin-pleads-guilty

ABOUT AUTHOR

Chris Krafft studied economics before going on to obtain a diploma in photojournalism. He has been fortunate to have lived and worked in numerous countries. When not writing, he can be found tinkering on boats and is an avid sailor. Read more of his writing on Substack: https://chriskrafft.substack.com

Printed in Great Britain
by Amazon